Popular Chinese Cookbook

Popular Chinese Cookbook

Alison Burt

Contents

Photograph on page 39 by courtesy of Syndication International
Photographs on pages 7, 15, 18–19, 23, 26–27, 47, 55, 71, 75, 79, 87, 94 by Barry Bullough
Accessories provided by Cheong-Leen Supermarket, London

Frontispiece: Prawns with vegetables and boiled rice

This edition first published 1977 by
Octopus Books Limited
59 Grosvenor Street, London W1

ISBN 0 7064 0629 X

© 1972, 1977 Octopus Books Limited

Produced by Mandarin Publishers Limited,
Hong Kong
Printed in Hong Kong

Weights and Measures

All measurements in this book are based on Imperial weights and measures, with American equivalents given in parenthesis.

Measurements in *weight* in the Imperial and American system are the same.
Measurements in *volume* are different, and the following table shows the equivalents:

Spoon measurements

Imperial	U.S.
1 teaspoon (5ml.)	$1\frac{1}{4}$ teaspoons
1 tablespoon (20ml.)	$1\frac{1}{4}$ tablespoons (abbrev: T)

Level spoon measurements are used in all the recipes.

Liquid measurements
1 Imperial pint . . . . 20 fluid ounces
1 American pint . . . . 16 fluid ounces
1 American cup. . . . . .8 fluid ounces

Introduction

The Chinese have always been inscrutable and, to most Westerners, so has their cookery. Although Chinese food is now enjoyed at many Chinese restaurants all over the country, cookery books are few, mainly, I believe, because the Chinese are very bad at writing down their recipes.

Chinese cooks make up their own recipes and seem to know instinctively how much of each ingredient to use. Even with the recipes in this book you can change the quantity of some ingredient or substitute one ingredient for another. You can, in fact, use these recipes as a 'stepping off' point from which you can develop your own initiative and inventiveness. The very essence of Chinese cooking is to use your own personal taste and ideas. Another thing that deters many people from trying to cook Chinese food is that they do not know where to buy the ingredients or if they come across an unusual ingredient, what to use as a substitute if it is unavailable.

Ingredients

Nearly all ingredients for Chinese cooking are available at larger supermarkets or grocery shops and health food stores sometimes stock a range of Chinese groceries. Those items which have to be purchased from shops specializing in Chinese foods are mostly canned or dried so you can stock up when visiting the shop or when ordering by post. If you have the following ingredients in your cupboard in addition to your normal shopping, you will be able to try any of the recipes in this book.

Bamboo Shoot

available canned from larger supermarkets. The sizes vary so use one nearest to that recommended in the recipe. Some cans have the bamboo shoot already sliced which is very convenient.

A SELECTION OF CHINESE INGREDIENTS AND UTENSILS

Bean Sprouts
available canned from larger supermarkets. The sizes vary so use one nearest to that recommended in the recipe. Fresh bean sprouts can be bought from Chinese food stores.

Black Beans (Chinese salted)
available canned from larger supermarkets.

Chow Chow
Canned Chinese preserved fruit, available from Chinese food stores.

Egg Noodles (Chinese dried)
available from larger supermarkets, in packets.

Five-spice Powder
available from Chinese food stores.

Ginger
Fresh ginger can be bought from good greengrocers or supermarkets.

Hoi Sin Sauce
available canned from Chinese food stores.

Lychees
available canned from larger supermarkets. They can sometimes be bought fresh.

Monosodium Glutamate
available from larger supermarkets. This white 'taste powder' is called Ac'cent in Britain and the U.S.A.; Zip in Australia.

Mushrooms
Chinese dried mushrooms are available from Chinese food stores. When fresh mushrooms are needed for a recipe, use small button mushrooms or canned champignons.

Oyster Sauce
available in cans from Chinese food stores.

Sesame Seeds
available from health food shops.

Shark's fin
available, dried, from Chinese food stores.

Soy Sauce
available from larger supermarkets.

Snow Peas
available from greengrocers or Chinese food stores when in season.

Star Anise
available from Chinese food stores.

Transparent Noodles
available from Chinese food stores in packets.

Water Chestnuts
available canned from larger supermarkets.

Preparing the Ingredients

All fresh ingredients should be of good quality and as fresh as possible. The majority of time, when making a Chinese dish, is spent preparing rather than actually cooking the food. Chinese cooking is usually done quickly and the food must be cooked through but remain crisp and succulent. The ingredients are mostly cut up into small pieces and if this is done correctly, the food will become tender more quickly and the dish will look more 'Chinese'! A Chinese cook uses a small chopper for cutting up vegetables, meat, poultry and so on, but a sharp kitchen knife will do these jobs just as well.

Cut *celery* diagonally by slanting the knife to a 45° angle and cutting the sticks in $\frac{1}{8}$-$\frac{1}{4}$ inch slices.

Cut *carrot* into wedges by first making a slanting cut across the carrot, then turning it $\frac{1}{3}$ turn away from you and making another slanting cut which comes halfway up the cut surface.

Cut *peppers* into wedges by removing the seeds and membranes, cutting the pepper into strips about $\frac{1}{2}$-$\frac{3}{4}$ inch wide then cutting these diagonally to make triangles. Matchstick strips should be approximately the shape and size of a matchstick.

Cut an *onion* into eighths by placing it on its end and, always cutting downwards, cutting it first in half, then in quarters, and finally into eighths.

Cut *spring onions* (*scallions*) in lengths across, not lengthways. Use about 1 inch of the green.

Cut *water chestnuts* in slices to make small rounds.

Cut *bamboo shoot* as for peppers.

When *crushed garlic* or *finely chopped fresh ginger* are used these ingredients should be almost a pulp.

When a recipe says 'cut *chicken* into eighths', chop it into pieces going right through the bones.

Chicken stock can be substituted with water and a chicken stock cube, except in making soup, when it is important that real stock is used. Frequently chicken dishes use chicken which is boiled first, in which case add a carrot and an onion to the water and use this stock when making the soup.

Beef stock can be substituted with water and beef stock cube except in making soup, when canned beef consommé should be used.

Peanut oil is more widely used in Chinese cooking than other oils. Maize oil, groundnut oil or sunflower seed oil may be used as substitutes, but you should never use olive oil. The oil is hot enough for deep frying when a thermometer reads 375°F, or when a $\frac{1}{2}$ inch cube of bread browns in the oil in less than a minute.

Meat should be cut across the grain to facilitate the quick cooking procedure.

Leftover ingredients will store well in sealed plastic containers in the refrigerator. Dry ingredients should be kept in a cool dry cupboard.

Utensils

The utensil most frequently used in Chinese cooking is a *wok*. This is a large concave pan with a rounded base. It is used for frying (deep and shallow), boiling and simmering, and has the advantage that the food may be pushed to the sides of the pan, allowing the liquid to drain down into the bowl. There is something rather pleasing about using a wok when preparing a Chinese meal, but you can easily use the saucepans and frying pans which you already have in your kitchen. Every Chinese kitchen has a steamer. If you do not own one, use a heatproof bowl or dish and stand it in or over a saucepan of gently simmering water – the result will be the same.

The Chinese use chopsticks for most cooking operations, but unless you are an expert, use a wooden spoon, a perforated kitchen spoon, a fish slice or a pair of kitchen tongs as appropriate. The flavour of Chinese food is very delicate and can easily be tainted with metal, so try to use wooden spoons and china or glass bowls to prevent the food from touching metal as much as possible.

Planning and Preparing a Meal

Planning a Chinese meal is half the fun. The Chinese like to have a variety of dishes for the main course, eating a little of each. I find it easiest to start with soup and then have four dishes to make up the main course, followed by a light dessert. All the recipes in the book state the number of people they will serve but this, of course, will vary according to the number of dishes to be served at a meal. If a recipe serves 4-6 people this means that it will serve four people if four dishes are served; six people if six dishes are served. For your first meal, plan four dishes for the main course, using a variety of ingredients and flavours. One of the dishes will be rice, then perhaps choose one chicken, one pork and one fish, egg or vegetable to make a wide variety. Most of the dishes are cooked on top of the cooker and I find it makes life much easier if I can include one dish which is cooked in the oven. Chinese food may be kept warming for quite a time without spoiling, except for food fried in batter which, naturally, will go soft if kept hot. Make sure that the dishes you choose can all be cooked ahead of time, leaving only one dish at the most which needs last minute cooking. Cover the food with aluminium foil to stop it from becoming dry while being kept warm.

Start preparing the food in good time. Be methodical. Collect all the ingredients together and a selection of saucepans and bowls to put the prepared food in. It is the chopping and cutting of the ingredients that takes time, the actual cooking time is usually very short. If the ingredients are to be marinated, leave them in the marinade until you are ready to cook. Every good Chinese cook washes up as he goes along and I would advise you to do the same; after the meal you will then have a minimum of dishes – even less than with a normal meal.

Garnishes should be prepared with the other ingredients. Sometimes an appropriate garnish is given with a recipe but otherwise use one or more of the following:

Toasted flaked almonds: Place the blanched and flaked almonds in the grill pan under a hot grill. Stir occasionally until golden brown.

Omelette: Beat one egg with salt and pepper. Heat a little oil in a small frying pan and make a thin omelette. Cut into long very thin strips with a sharp knife. Small whole omelettes, about 2 inches in diameter, can also be used.

Spring onion (scallion) flowers: cut a $1\frac{1}{2}$-2 inch length of the green part of a spring onion (scallion). Push out the middle and, using the outside only, snip $\frac{1}{2}$ inch cuts into each end of the spring onion (scallion) about $\frac{1}{8}$-$\frac{1}{4}$ inch apart. Drop each 'flower' into iced water and the snipped ends will curl backwards.

Chopped green spring onion (scallion) top.

Parsley, or Chinese parsley which is not so curly: Chop, or use sprigs.

Watercress, or Chinese watercress, which has thicker leaves: Use in big sprigs.

Transparent noodles: Fry in deep hot oil until puffed up – about 5 seconds. Drain well.

Some menus to try

For 4 people

Prawn (Shrimp) and Egg Flower Soup	Raindrop Soup
Fried Rice	Party Fried Rice
Chicken with Lychees	Crisp Skin Chicken
Pork with Bean Sprouts and Almonds	Shredded Lamb with Onions
Crisp Skin Fish	Golden Braised Fish
Almond Cream with Chow Chow	Gingered Fruits

For 5-6 people

Beef and Vegetable Soup	Wun Tun Soup
Boiled Rice	Fried Rice
Braised Duck with Sweet and Pungent Sauce	Chicken Chop Suey
Beef Chow Mein	Red Roast Pork
Mixed Omelette	Braised Cabbage with Mushrooms

Spring Rolls	Wun Tuns
Almond Biscuits or Caramel Bananas	Mow Flower Twists or Almond Lake with Mandarin Oranges

Entertaining

To entertain your friends Chinese-style is great fun, and since you are preparing and cooking this food, why not serve it in true traditional Chinese fashion? The Chinese are very good at giving feasts – they often have up to 32 courses. They can, however, equally have only three or four, which is much simpler to prepare – especially if you are doing all the cooking yourself.

Plan the menu and prepare the food as suggested in the Introduction. In addition, place small bowls on the table, before the meal begins, with salted nuts, glacé fruits (pineapple, figs, apricots etc.), pickles and any other small delicacies. These appetizers stay on the table throughout the meal, and the guests nibble at them as they please. For a big feast, have about twelve bowls, but for a more modest meal, four to six would be quite adequate.

Set the table, placing a large plate or dish and a small bowl for each person – and a pair of chopsticks (it might be wise to have a fork too!). If soup is to be served, supply a Chinese spoon for each person. This is made of porcelain, which, unlike metal, doesn't get very hot and burn your lips, nor does it taint the very delicate flavour of your carefully prepared soup! All the food is brought to the table in large serving dishes, so put plenty of serving spoons on the table, not forgetting the soup ladle. The Chinese serve the dishes one after the other, but this is not very practical for the Western housewife and so it has become the custom to serve the soup first, followed by all the remaining savoury dishes. The guests help themselves to the food and come back for more as they want it. The meal may last for quite a long time, so it is a good idea to have small food warmers (either electrically heated or using small candles) on the table to keep the food hot.

If you are really going to follow the Chinese style of entertaining, place your guest of honour at the end of the table, facing the door, and arrange the rest of the guests so that the least important is sitting beside the host, who will have his back to the door. Place husbands and wives next to each other, as it is the custom that the ladies depend on their husbands to serve them with food. This usually means that the ladies get all the best and most succulent foods, for who would serve a lady anything but the best!

The soup is eaten from the small bowl, which is then used to put the rice in for the second course. The same plate can be used throughout the meal, but may be changed for the dessert.

Chopsticks are the normal table implements in China. Wooden, plastic of bamboo chopsticks are for everyday use, but for a feast, ivory is preferred. There are many superstitions about chopsticks, one being that it is bad luck to drop them, and another that if you find you have an unmatched pair you will miss your aeroplane, ship or train! So beware – but use them in the correct way and all should be well. Hold the chopsticks just above halfway up. The lower stick should always remain still. It is held between the second and third fingers, and rests on the knuckle of the first finger, kept in place with the thumb. The upper stick is used as a lever for picking up food. Make sure that the ends of the chopsticks are level; hold the upper stick between the tips of the second and third fingers and support it with the ball of the thumb. It takes quite a lot of practice, but if you differentiate between food that is actually picked up between the chopsticks and food that is scooped up on to them, such as rice, you will be more successful.

China Tea. This is served throughout a Chinese meal. It is pale in colour, very scented and extremely refreshing. Keep a special teapot for making China tea and always warm the pot before putting the tea in. Allow 1 teaspoon of tea for each person present, use freshly boiled water and allow the tea leaves to infuse for 3-5 minutes before pouring. Never add milk or sugar to China tea. It is at its best when freshly made, so if you are going to serve it right through a meal, make a fresh pot very frequently.

Chinese Hot-Pot

All the recipes in this book are ideal to serve as part of a feast. For a very special occasion, however, or for something completely different, try serving your guests a Chinese Hot-pot. As well as being delicious to eat, this is also a most attractive meal to present. Chinese fire kettles, especially made for cooking this meal, are available from Chinese stores. They are heated with charcoal and look most impressive on the dining table. You can, however, use a small adjustable spirit burner and place on top an attractive saucepan or fondue pot.

Place the small dishes of appetizers on the table, and on a large platter, arrange a selection of very thin slices of raw meat (fillet steak, lamb's kidney and liver, veal kidney), whole prawns (shrimps), sliced scallops and fish fillets, and bite-size pieces of cooked chicken. Allow a total of about 6 oz. of meat and fish for each person. Also serve rice, fried or boiled, and a crisp salad such as Sesame and Chicken Salad (see recipes pages 80, 82–83). A selection of Chinese sauces (the recipes for which are given on page 16) should also be served.

Fill the saucepan or fondue pot – or fire kettle – with boiling chicken stock. Place this on the burner and adjust the flame to keep the stock simmering. Add a ½ inch slice of fresh ginger. The guests serve themselves with rice and salad, then select a piece of meat, fish or chicken with chopsticks (or fork!) and dip it in the simmering stock, until it is cooked – about 1-2 minutes. The cooked food is then dipped into a sauce and, finally, eaten. You will find that everyone will soon become their own expert cook.

When all the meat has been cooked and eaten, add to the stock about 2-4 tablespoons of sherry (according to taste) and salt and pepper to taste and serve this to your guests in soup bowls – it is absolutely delicious. A light dessert may follow but this is not normal.

Sauces for Chinese Hot-Pot

Soy and Garlic Sauce: Place $\frac{1}{4}$ pint ($\frac{5}{8}$ cup) of soy sauce in a small saucepan with 2 crushed cloves of garlic. Bring to the boil, simmer for 2 minutes. Serve warm or cold.

Soy and Ginger Sauce: Place $\frac{1}{4}$ pint ($\frac{5}{8}$ cup) of soy sauce in a saucepan with 2 teaspoons of very finely chopped fresh ginger and a pinch of freshly ground black pepper. Bring to the boil and simmer for 2 minutes. Serve warm or cold.

Sweet and Sour Sauce: Place 2 tablespoons ($2\frac{1}{2}$ T) of vinegar and 2 tablespoons ($2\frac{1}{2}$ T) of brown sugar in a small saucepan with 1 tablespoon ($1\frac{1}{4}$ T) of cornflour and salt and pepper to taste. Mix well and stir in $\frac{1}{4}$ pint ($\frac{5}{8}$ cup) of chicken stock and 1 teaspoon of tomato paste. Bring to the boil, stirring constantly, and simmer for 2-3 minutes. Serve warm.

Plum sauce: Plum sauce is available canned from Chinese food stores. To make it at home, mix together 6 tablespoons ($7\frac{1}{2}$ T) of sieved plum jam, 3 tablespoons ($3\frac{3}{4}$ T) of chopped mango chutney, 1 tablespoon ($1\frac{1}{4}$ T) of vinegar, 2 teaspoons of sugar and salt and pepper to taste. Beat well and serve cold.

Hoi Sin Sauce: Available canned from Chinese food stores. Serve cold.

Vinegar and Ginger Sauce: Mix all the following ingredients together thoroughly: 1 tablespoon ($1\frac{1}{4}$ T) of very finely chopped fresh ginger, 1 crushed clove of garlic, 4 tablespoons (5 T) of vinegar, 1 teaspoon of sugar, pinch of monosodium glutamate, 1 teaspoon of tomato paste, salt and pepper to taste. Serve cold.

Soups

Chinese soups have an extremely delicate flavour which depends almost entirely on the quality of the stock used. In a Chinese kitchen there is a pot of chicken stock constantly ready for use. Do not substitute with water and a chicken cube but try to incorporate a chicken dish in the menu, for which the chicken has to be boiled. Add a carrot, an onion, a few peppercorns and the giblets to the cooking water which, after the chicken has cooked, may be strained and makes a good stock for soup. Beef stock also must not be substituted with water and a beef stock cube. If you have no home-made stock ready, use canned beef consommé.
Always serve Chinese soup piping hot.

Beef and Vegetable Soup

4 oz. beef (topside)
1 tomato
2 spring onions (scallions)
6 water chestnuts
$\frac{1}{2}$ × 8 oz. can bamboo shoot

4 Chinese dried mushrooms
$1\frac{1}{2}$ pints (3$\frac{3}{4}$ cups) beef stock
pinch of monosodium
  glutamate
salt and pepper

Cut the beef into thin strips across the grain of the meat. Skin the tomato and slice into 4. Slice the spring onions (scallions), water chestnuts and bamboo shoots into thin strips. Soak the mushrooms in warm water for 20 minutes, rinse, squeeze dry and cut into thin strips, discarding the stalks. Put the stock into a large saucepan and bring to the boil. Add the beef and simmer for 4-5 minutes. Add the vegetables and cook for 2 minutes. Add the monosodium glutamate and season to taste.
Serve very hot.
Serves 4-6

Mushroom Soup

2 spring onions (scallions)
4 oz. button mushrooms
1½ pints (3¾ cups) chicken
   stock
½ inch slice fresh ginger
1 tablespoon (1¼ T) sherry
salt and pepper

Slice, thinly, the spring onions (scallions) and button mushrooms. Put the stock in a saucepan with the ginger and spring onions. Bring to the boil and simmer, covered, for 20 minutes.

Add the mushrooms and simmer for a further 10 minutes. Remove the ginger. Add the sherry and season to taste. Serve very hot.

Serves 4-6

Prawn (Shrimp) and Egg Flower Soup

2 spring onions (scallions)
1½ pints (3¾ cups) chicken
   stock
½ tablespoon dry sherry
pinch of monosodium
   glutamate
pinch of sugar
1 teaspoon soy sauce
6 oz. (1½ cups) peeled prawns
   (shrimps)
1 egg, well beaten
salt

Chop the spring onions (scallions) finely and put them into a large saucepan with the stock. Bring to the boil and simmer, covered, for 10 minutes.

Add the sherry, monosodium glutamate, sugar, soy sauce and prawns (shrimps). Reheat gently until the prawns (shrimps) are heated through.

Pour in the egg and stir until it separates into shreds. Add salt to taste.

Serve immediately.

Note: King prawns should be deveined and cut in half.

Serves 4-6

Wun Tun Soup

Either buy ready made wun tun skins from a shop which specializes in Chinese groceries, or make your own, using ¼ of the quantities in the recipe given on page 84.

1½ pints (3¾ cups) chicken stock
salt and pepper
4 oz. (1 cup) chopped cooked chicken
4 oz. (1 cup) peeled prawns (shrimps)

2 spring onions (scallions)
8 wun tun skins
1 egg white
snipped green tops of spring onions (scallions)

Put the stock in a large saucepan and heat slowly until boiling, seasoning to taste.
Chop the chicken, prawns (shrimps) and spring onions (scallions) very very finely and mix them together. Place some of this filling on each wun tun skin, moisten the edges with a little egg white and fold over like a small turnover. Press the edges together well.
Drop the wun tuns into the boiling stock and cook for about 10 minutes.
Serve sprinkled with snipped green spring onion (scallion) tops.
Serves 8

Raindrop Soup

6 water chestnuts
2 spring onions (scallions)
1 tablespoon (1¼ T) sherry
salt and pepper

1½ pints (3¾ cups) chicken stock
6 oz. (1½ cups) diced cooked chicken

Slice the water chestnuts and slice the spring onions (scallions) finely. Put these into a saucepan with the chicken stock and the chicken. Bring to the boil and simmer, covered, for 15 minutes.
Add the sherry and season to taste.
Serve very hot.
Serves 4-6

Fish

Fish is widely eaten in China, especially in the coastal areas. The fish used in Chinese cooking should always be very fresh and this is considered so important that in Chinese food stores the fish are often alive, swimming in large barrels.

At least one fish dish is usually included in the main course if you are entertaining Chinese style. Frequently this is shellfish, as the delicate flavours of prawns (shrimps), scallops, crab and so on lend themselves to Chinese cooking. If you are able to buy 'green' or uncooked prawns use these in preference to the ready cooked ones.

Fish Rolls with Walnuts

This dish makes an ideal appetizer, either to begin the meal or served with drinks beforehand.

2 large fish fillets (John Dory, Flounder, Plaice or Sole)
2 spring onions (scallions)
$\frac{1}{2}$ teaspoon salt
$\frac{1}{2}$ teaspoon sugar
$\frac{1}{2}$ teaspoon cornflour (cornstarch)
1 teaspoon soy sauce
1 teaspoon dry sherry
1 egg
2 oz. ($\frac{1}{2}$ cup) walnuts, very finely chopped or ground
2 × 1 oz. slices cooked ham
8 wooden cocktail sticks
oil for deep frying

Cut the fillets into quarters, making 8 even-sized pieces.
Chop the spring onions (scallions) finely, mix with salt, sugar, cornflour (cornstarch), soy sauce, sherry and egg and beat together well.
Dip the fish pieces in the egg mixture and then in the walnuts.
Cut each slice of ham in quarters and lay a quarter on each piece of fish. Roll up and secure with a cocktail stick.
Deep fry in hot oil until golden. Drain well on absorbent kitchen paper.
Serve very hot.
Serves 4-6

Fish in Sweet and Sour Sauce

1 lb. fish fillets
1 carrot
1 green pepper
2 sticks celery
3 tomatoes
3 tablespoons ($3\frac{3}{4}$ T) peanut oil
4 tablespoons (5 T) vinegar

4 tablespoons (5 T) sugar
1 teaspoon very finely
    chopped fresh ginger
$\frac{1}{2}$ teaspoon salt
$\frac{1}{2}$ tablespoon cornflour
    (cornstarch)

Skin the fish and cut it into bite-sized pieces. Cut the carrot
and pepper into matchstick strips. Cut the celery diagonally.
Drop the prepared vegetables into boiling water and simmer
for 5 minutes. Drain.

Skin the tomatoes, remove seeds and chop roughly. Heat the
oil in a small pan and fry the fish until cooked, about 5-7
minutes. Remove the fish and drain.

Pour off excess oil, add the vinegar, sugar, ginger, salt,
cornflour (cornstarch), all the vegetables and $\frac{1}{4}$ pint ($\frac{5}{8}$ cup) of
water. Bring to the boil, stirring, add the fish and simmer for
2 minutes.

Serve in a heated dish.

Serves 4-6

Sesame Fish

Sesame fish can also be served as a delicious appetizer.

1 lb. fish fillets
1 teaspoon very finely
    chopped fresh ginger
1 onion
2 tablespoons ($2\frac{1}{2}$ T) dry
    sherry
$\frac{1}{2}$ teaspoon salt
pinch of pepper

1 teaspoon sugar
1 oz. ($\frac{1}{4}$ cup) cornflour
    (cornstarch)
1 oz. ($\frac{1}{4}$ cup) plain flour
1 egg
sesame seeds
oil for deep frying

Skin the fish and cut into bite-sized pieces. Chop the onion
finely and mix together in a bowl with the ginger, sherry, salt,
pepper and sugar. Add the fish pieces and marinate for 10
minutes, stirring occasionally. Drain.

24

Sift the cornflour and flour into a bowl. Add egg, 3 table-spoons water and mix well. Dip fish in this batter, then in sesame seeds. Deep fry in hot oil until crisp and golden. Serve hot.
Serves 4-6

Crisp Skin Fish

4 whiting
4 oz. (1 cup) peeled prawns (shrimps)
4 Chinese dried mushrooms
1 spring onion (scallion)
1 teaspoon very finely chopped fresh ginger
salt
1 egg yolk
cornflour (cornstarch)

oil for frying
1 tablespoon ($1\frac{1}{4}$ T) vinegar
1 tablespoon ($1\frac{1}{4}$ T) sugar
2 tablespoons ($2\frac{1}{2}$ T) Chinese black beans
1 tablespoon ($1\frac{1}{4}$ T) cornflour (cornstarch)
$\frac{1}{4}$ pint ($\frac{5}{8}$ cup) fish stock or water
1 tablespoon ($1\frac{1}{4}$ T) soy sauce

Clean the whiting, leaving on the heads and tails. Chop the prawns (shrimps) and spring onions (scallions). Soak the mushrooms for 20 minutes, rinse, squeeze dry, and chop, discarding the stalks.
Mix the prawns (shrimps), mushrooms, spring onions (scallions) and ginger and stuff each fish with this mixture. Sew up the openings. Rub salt into gashes cut on both sides of each fish in the thickest part.
Beat the egg yolk with 1 teaspoon of water and brush over the fish. When nearly dry, rub over the cornflour (cornstarch). Heat about 2 inches of oil in a pan and fry the fish, turning once. When cooked, drain on absorbent paper. Keep hot.
Place all the remaining ingredients in a small saucepan with salt to taste. Bring to the boil, stirring constantly, and simmer for 2-3 minutes. Place the fish on a hot serving plate, pour the sauce over and serve.
Serves 4-8

CRISP SKIN FISH IN PREPARATION

Butterfly Prawns with Celery and Mushrooms

1 lb. king prawns (shrimps), peeled
2 oz. ($\frac{1}{2}$ cup) self raising (all purpose) flour
pinch of salt
4 fl. oz. ($\frac{1}{2}$ cup) water
$\frac{1}{2}$ teaspoon vinegar
4 Chinese dried mushrooms
4 sticks celery
1 tablespoon ($1\frac{1}{4}$ T) peanut oil
1 clove garlic, crushed
2 teaspoons soy sauce
1 tablespoon ($1\frac{1}{4}$ T) dry sherry
salt and pepper to taste
oil for deep frying

Remove the dark vein from the back of each prawn (shrimp) and cut nearly, but not quite, in half lengthways. Open them out like butterflies and press open between the palms of your hands.

Sift the flour and salt into a bowl and mix in water and vinegar to make a smooth batter.

Soak mushrooms in warm water for 20 minutes, rinse, squeeze dry, and slice thinly, discarding the stalks. Slice the celery diagonally.

Heat the oil in a small saucepan and add the garlic, mushrooms, and celery. Fry, stirring, for 3 minutes. Add the sherry, soy sauce, seasonings and 4 tablespoons of water.

Dip the prawns (shrimps) into the batter and deep fry in hot oil until golden. Drain on absorbent kitchen paper. Reheat the sauce.

Serve immediately, with the sauce poured over the prawns (shrimps).

Serves 4-6

Prawn (Shrimp) Chop Suey

8 oz. (2 cups) peeled prawns (shrimps)
4 Chinese dried mushrooms
1 × 16 oz. can bean sprouts
$\frac{1}{2}$ × 8 oz. can bamboo shoot
8 water chestnuts
$\frac{1}{2}$ tablespoon cornflour (cornstarch)
pinch of salt
1 tablespoon ($1\frac{1}{4}$ T) soy sauce
1 clove garlic, crushed
1 teaspoon sugar
1 tablespoon ($1\frac{1}{4}$ T) dry sherry
2 oz. ($\frac{1}{2}$ cup) blanched toasted almonds

Prepare the prawns (shrimps), cutting the large ones in half.
Soak the mushrooms in warm water for 20 minutes, rinse,
squeeze dry and slice, discarding the stalks. Rinse the bean
sprouts under running cold water. Drain. Cut the bamboo
shoot and water chestnuts into matchstick strips.
Mix the cornflour (cornstarch), salt, soy sauce, garlic, sugar,
sherry, vegetables and 4 tablespoons of water in a small saucepan.
Bring to the boil and simmer slowly, stirring, for 2-3 minutes.
Stir in the prawns (shrimps), cover the pan and reheat gently.
Serve on a heated serving dish topped with the almonds.
Note Toast the almonds by heating under a hot grill, stirring
occasionally until golden.
Serves 4-6

Golden Braised Fish

1 × 2 lb. whole fish (Bream, Bass or Snapper are suitable)
salt
plain flour
4 Chinese dried mushrooms
4 spring onions (scallions)
oil for frying
1 teaspoon very finely chopped fresh ginger

$\frac{1}{2}$ pint (1$\frac{1}{4}$ cups) fish stock or water
2 tablespoons (2$\frac{1}{2}$ T) soy sauce
1 tablespoon (1$\frac{1}{4}$ T) sherry
1 teaspoon salt
6 water chestnuts
2 cloves garlic, crushed
1 clove star anise
1 teaspoon sugar

Clean the fish, leaving on the head and tail. Wipe inside and
out with kitchen paper. Make 2 gashes on each side, in the
thickest part. Sprinkle with salt and coat in flour. Soak the
mushrooms in warm water for 20 minutes, rinse, squeeze dry
and discard stalks. Cut the mushrooms into strips and the
spring onions (scallions) into $\frac{1}{2}$ inch lengths. Slice the water
chestnuts.
Heat a little oil in a large frying pan and, when hot, fry the
fish on both sides until golden. Pour off excess oil and add the
mushrooms, spring onions (scallions), ginger, stock, soy sauce,
sherry, salt, water chestnuts, garlic, star anise and sugar.
Cover the pan, bring to the boil and simmer for about 30
minutes, turning the fish once.
Serve on a large heated plate with the sauce poured over.
Serves 4-6

Sweet and Sour Prawns (Shrimps)

8 oz. (2 cups) peeled prawns
  (shrimps)
1 tablespoon ($1\frac{1}{4}$ T) sherry
salt and pepper
1 onion
1 green pepper
1 tablespoon ($1\frac{1}{4}$ T) peanut oil
$\frac{1}{2} \times 15$ oz. can pineapple
  chunks

1 tablespoon ($1\frac{1}{4}$ T) cornflour
  (cornstarch)
1 tablespoon ($1\frac{1}{4}$ T) soy sauce
$\frac{1}{4}$ pint ($\frac{5}{8}$ cup) vinegar
4 tablespoons (5 T) brown
  sugar

Place the prawns (shrimps) in a bowl with the sherry and seasonings and marinate for 1 hour.

Slice the onion and cut the pepper into wedges. Put the oil in a small saucepan, add the vegetables, and fry gently until softened. Add the pineapple.

Mix together the cornflour (cornstarch), soy sauce, vinegar and sugar and add these to the saucepan. Bring to the boil, stirring constantly, and simmer for 2-3 minutes. Add the prawns (shrimps) and sherry and reheat.

Serve in a heated bowl.

Serves 4-6

Prawns (Shrimps) with Vegetables

1 lb. prawns (shrimps), peeled
1 red pepper
2 sticks celery
2 Chinese dried mushrooms
2 spring onions (scallions)
6 water chestnuts
1 tablespoon ($1\frac{1}{4}$ T) cornflour
  (cornstarch)
1 tablespoon ($1\frac{1}{4}$ T) soy sauce
pinch of sugar

1 tablespoon ($1\frac{1}{4}$ T) peanut oil
$\frac{1}{2}$ teaspoon very finely
  chopped fresh ginger
1 clove garlic, crushed
$\frac{1}{2}$ teaspoon salt
2 pineapple rings, chopped
  (optional)
$\frac{1}{2}$ pint ($1\frac{1}{4}$ cups) chicken stock
1 oz. ($\frac{1}{4}$ cup) flaked toasted
  almonds

Prepare the prawns (shrimps). If using large prawns (shrimps), devein them and cut them in half.

Cut the pepper in matchstick strips and slice the celery

diagonally. Soak the mushrooms in warm water for 20 minutes, rinse and squeeze dry, discarding the stalks, and slice. Cut the spring onions (scallions) in $\frac{1}{2}$ inch pieces and slice the water chestnuts. Mix the cornflour (cornstarch) with soy sauce, sugar and 2 tablespoons of water.

Heat the oil and add the ginger, garlic and salt. Add the prepared vegetables, pineapple and stock. Bring to the boil and simmer, stirring, for 5 minutes. Add the cornflour mixture and cook, stirring, for 2-3 minutes. Add the prawns and allow just to heat through.

Serve in a hot serving dish, scattered with flaked toasted almonds.

Note: Toast flaked almonds by heating under a hot grill, stirring occasionally, until golden.

Serves 4-6

Prawn (Shrimp) Balls

4 oz. (1 cup) self raising
  (all purpose) flour
1 egg
$\frac{1}{4}$ pint ($\frac{5}{8}$ cup) water
pinch of salt
1 lb. peeled king prawns
  (shrimps)

2 tablespoons ($2\frac{1}{2}$ T) cornflour
  (cornstarch)
$\frac{1}{2}$ teaspoon salt
$\frac{1}{2}$ teaspoon white pepper
pinch monosodium glutamate
peanut oil for deep frying
parsley sprigs for garnish

Sift the flour and salt into a bowl. Make a well in the centre and add the egg. Using a wooden spoon, mix the flour into the egg, add half the water and continue mixing, drawing in the flour. Beat thoroughly and stir in remaining water.

Cut the prawns (shrimps) into chunks about 1 inch across. Mix the cornflour (cornstarch) with the remaining salt, pepper and monosodium glutamate. Coat the prawn (shrimp) pieces in seasoned cornflour (cornstarch). Dip the prawns (shrimps) in batter and fry in deep, hot oil until crisp and golden. Drain well on absorbent kitchen paper.

Serve hot, garnished with sprigs of parsley.

Serves 4-6

Pineapple Fish

1 lb. fish fillet (haddock or snapper) or 2 × 7 oz. cans tuna

4 oz. (1 cup) self raising (all purpose) flour

pinch of salt

1 egg

$\frac{1}{4}$ pint ($\frac{5}{8}$ cup) water

pinch of monosodium glutamate

4 pineapple rings

2 tablespoons ($2\frac{1}{2}$ T) soft brown sugar

1 tablespoon ($1\frac{1}{4}$ T) cornflour (cornstarch)

2 tablespoons ($2\frac{1}{2}$ T) vinegar

1 tablespoon ($1\frac{1}{4}$ T) soy sauce

1 teaspoon very finely chopped fresh ginger

$\frac{1}{4}$ pint ($\frac{5}{8}$ cup) syrup from canned pineapple

salt to taste

toasted flaked almonds for garnish

oil for deep frying

Skin the fish and cut into bite-sized pieces or drain the tuna and break into bite-sized pieces.

Sift the flour and salt together into a mixing bowl. Make a well in the centre, add the egg and mix with a little flour, using a wooden spoon. Gradually add the water, then the flour, and beat until the batter is smooth. Beat in the monosodium glutamate.

Chop the pineapple roughly. Mix together the brown sugar, cornflour (cornstarch), vinegar, soy sauce, ginger, pineapple syrup, salt and $\frac{1}{4}$ pint ($\frac{5}{8}$ cup) of water. Bring to the boil, stirring, and boil for 2-3 minutes.

Dip the fish pieces in batter and fry in deep hot oil until crisp and golden. Drain on absorbent kitchen paper. Add the pineapple pieces to the sauce and reheat.

Sprinkle the fish with the toasted flaked almonds and serve in a hot serving bowl with the sauce poured over.

Serves 4-6

PINEAPPLE FISH (*Photograph: John West*)

Meat

Pork is the meat most commonly eaten in China, except where religion forbids it, when beef is eaten instead. Use the best possible cuts of meat and always slice it across the grain which helps to make it more tender for the Chinese-style quick cooking. Although the meat may be expensive, a little goes a long way, and each dish works out to be quite economical.

Pork with Chicken and Vegetables

$\frac{1}{2}$ lb. spring or shoulder (picnic shoulder) pork
$\frac{1}{4}$ lb. chicken
1 small red pepper
1 onion
2 sticks celery
6 water chestnuts
1 × 5 oz. can bamboo shoot
2 oz. button mushrooms

2 tablespoons ($2\frac{1}{2}$ T) peanut oil
1 tablespoon ($1\frac{1}{4}$ T) soy sauce
$\frac{1}{4}$ pint ($\frac{5}{8}$ cup) chicken stock
salt and pepper
1 tablespoon ($1\frac{1}{4}$ T) cornflour (cornstarch)
4 oz. Chinese dried egg noodles

Cut the pork and the chicken into thin strips. Cut the pepper into matchstick strips and the onion into eighths. Slice the celery diagonally and the water chestnuts and bamboo shoot into thin slices. Wipe and slice the mushrooms.

Heat the oil in a saucepan and fry the pork and chicken until they change colour, stirring constantly. Add the vegetables and fry, stirring, for 2-3 minutes. Pour off excess oil. Add the soy sauce, stock and seasonings and simmer for 5-7 minutes. Mix the cornflour (cornstarch) with a little water, add to the pan and simmer, stirring, for 2-3 minutes.

Cook the noodles in boiling salted water for 15 minutes. Drain. Serve with sauce poured over the noodles.

Serves 4-6

Sweet and Sour Pork with Lychees

1 lb. spring or shoulder (picnic shoulder) pork
3 tablespoons ($3\frac{3}{4}$ T) soy sauce
1 tablespoon ($1\frac{1}{4}$ T) dry sherry
1 teaspoon very finely chopped fresh ginger
pinch of monosodium glutamate
1 oz. ($\frac{1}{4}$ cup) plain flour
1 oz. ($\frac{1}{4}$ cup) cornflour (cornstarch)
pinch of salt
2 eggs, beaten
oil for deep frying
$\frac{1}{2}$ red pepper

$\frac{1}{2}$ green pepper
2 apples
1 tablespoon ($1\frac{1}{4}$ T) brown sugar
$\frac{1}{4}$ pint ($\frac{5}{8}$ cup) syrup from canned lychees
2 tablespoons ($2\frac{1}{2}$ T) vinegar
4 spring onions (scallions), finely chopped
1 × 11 oz. can lychees, drained
extra 1 tablespoon ($1\frac{1}{4}$ T) cornflour (cornstarch)
extra 1 tablespoon ($1\frac{1}{4}$ T) soy sauce
salt to taste

Cut the pork into 1 inch cubes. Mix together in a bowl the soy sauce, sherry, ginger and monosodium glutamate. Add the pork, stir to coat and marinate for 1-2 hours.

Sift the plain flour, cornflour (cornstarch) and salt into a bowl. Add the eggs gradually, beating well, to make a smooth batter. Coat the pork cubes in batter and deep fry in hot oil until golden. Drain on absorbent kitchen paper and keep hot. Cut the peppers into wedges. Peel, core and quarter the apples. Mix with all the remaining ingredients in a small saucepan. Bring to the boil, stirring constantly, and simmer for 2-3 minutes.

Put the pork on a heated serving dish and pour the sauce over. Serve as soon as possible.

Serves 4-6

Crispy Pork

1 lb. lean pork
2 tablespoons ($2\frac{1}{2}$ T) soy sauce
1 tablespoon ($1\frac{1}{4}$ T) sugar
1 clove star anise
1 tablespoon ($1\frac{1}{4}$ T) sherry
   (optional)
pinch of monosodium
   glutamate

4 oz. (1 cup) self raising (all
   purpose) flour
pinch of salt
1 egg
oil for frying

Cut the pork into 1 inch cubes. Put them in a saucepan with $\frac{3}{4}$ pint (approx. 2 cups) of water, soy sauce, sugar, star aniseed, sherry and monosodium glutamate. Simmer until tender, about 45 minutes. Drain well.

Sift the flour and salt into a bowl. Make a well in the centre, drop in the egg and mix with a wooden spoon, gradually bringing in the flour from around the edge. Add $\frac{1}{4}$ pint ($\frac{5}{8}$ cup) of water gradually, beating continually. Add the pork pieces and stir to coat in batter.

Heat oil in a frying pan and deep fry the coated pork pieces until crisp and golden. Drain well on absorbent kitchen paper. Serve as soon as possible.

Serves 4-6

Pork with Sweet and Pungent Sauce

1 lb. shoulder or spring (picnic shoulder) pork
4 tablespoons (5 T) soy sauce
2 cloves star anise
1 tablespoon ($1\frac{1}{4}$ T) brown sugar
$\frac{3}{4}$ pint (approx. 2 cups) chicken stock
1 carrot
1 small red or green pepper
4 pineapple rings

2 tablespoons ($2\frac{1}{2}$ T) brown sugar
2 tablespoons ($2\frac{1}{2}$ T) vinegar
1 teaspoon very finely chopped fresh ginger
1 clove garlic, crushed
1 tablespoon tomato paste
$\frac{1}{2}$ teaspoon salt
1 tablespoon ($1\frac{1}{4}$ T) dry sherry
1 tablespoon ($1\frac{1}{4}$ T) cornflour

Cut pork into long thin strips. Mix marinade of soy sauce, star aniseed, brown sugar and chicken stock. Marinate the pork for about 2 hours. Pour the pork and marinade into a saucepan, bring to the boil, stirring constantly, simmer for 20 minutes and drain.

Cut the carrot and pepper into wedges, drop into a saucepan of boiling water and simmer for 5 minutes. Drain. Cut pineapple rings into eighths. Place pork, vegetables, pineapple, $\frac{1}{4}$ pint water and all remaining ingredients into a saucepan. Bring to the boil, stirring constantly and simmer for 3-4 minutes.

Serves 4-6

Beef with Broccoli on Noodles

$\frac{3}{4}$ lb. topside or rump steak
2 onions
4 oz. Chinese dried egg
  noodles
1 teaspoon very finely
  chopped fresh ginger
1 tablespoon ($1\frac{1}{4}$ T) soy sauce
1 tablespoon ($1\frac{1}{4}$ T) oil
1 teaspoon sugar

$\frac{1}{2}$ teaspoon salt
pinch of monosodium
  glutamate
pinch of pepper
2 tablespoons ($2\frac{1}{2}$ T) cornflour
  (cornstarch)
$\frac{1}{4}$ pint ($\frac{5}{8}$ cup) beef stock
8 oz. cooked broccoli
oil for deep frying

Cut the beef into thin strips about 2 inches × $\frac{1}{4}$ inch × $\frac{1}{4}$ inch.
Cut the onions into eighths. Cook the noodles in boiling water
for 5 minutes, then drain very well. Place the meat in a bowl,
add ginger and soy sauce and marinate for 30 minutes.
Heat the oil in a saucepan and fry the beef, stirring constantly,
until it has changed colour. Mix together the sugar, salt,
monosodium glutamate, pepper, cornflour (cornstarch) and
beef stock, stir well and add to the pan. Bring to the boil,
stirring, add the onions and simmer for 5 minutes. Add the
broccoli and cook 4–5 minutes.
Deep fry the noodles in hot oil until golden. Drain well on
absorbent paper.
Serve the noodles on a heated dish, topped with the beef and
broccoli.
Serves 4-6

Pork with Bean Sprouts and Almonds

¾ lb. shoulder or spring (picnic shoulder) pork
1 × 16 oz. can bean sprouts
2 oz. (½ cup) blanched almonds
1 tablespoon (1¼ T) soy sauce
2 tablespoon (2½ T) chicken stock
1 teaspoon sugar
2 tablespoons (2½ T) peanut oil
2 spring onions (scallions), thinly sliced
1 pineapple ring, chopped
salt and pepper

Cut the pork into ½ inch cubes. Drain the bean sprouts, rinse in cold running water and drain again. Halve the almonds. Mix together the soy sauce, chicken stock and sugar.
Heat the oil in a frying pan and fry the pork, stirring, until it changes colour. Add the almonds and spring onions (scallions) and fry for 3-4 minutes. Pour off any oil. Add all the other ingredients, including the bean sprouts. Combine thoroughly, cover the pan and cook for 2 minutes.
Serves 4-6

Beef Chow Mein

¾ lb. topside or rump steak
1 teaspoon salt
2 teaspoons sugar
1 tablespoon (1¼ T) soy sauce
pinch of monosodium
    glutamate
4 Chinese dried mushrooms
1 × 16 oz. can bean sprouts
½ × 5 oz. can bamboo shoot
4 spring onions (scallions)

2 tablespoons (2½ T) cornflour
    (cornstarch)
¾ pint (approx. 2 cups) beef
    stock
3 tablespoons (3¾ T) peanut oil
4 oz. Chinese dried egg
    noodles
oil for deep frying
1 egg, beaten

Cut the beef into long strips, about 2 inches × ¼ inch × ¼ inch.
Mix together in a bowl the salt, sugar, soy sauce and
monosodium glutamate. Marinate the beef in this for 30
minutes.
Soak the mushrooms in warm water for 20 minutes, rinse,
squeeze dry and slice, discarding the stalks. Drain the bean
sprouts, rinse in cold running water and drain again. Slice
the bamboo shoot into thin strips. Cut the spring onions
(scallions) into 1 inch lengths. Mix the cornflour (cornstarch)
and stock together.
Drain the beef and reserve any remaining marinade. Heat the
oil in a pan and fry the beef, stirring, for about 3-4 minutes.
Add the marinade and the stock and cornflour (cornstarch)
mixture. Bring to the boil, stirring constantly, add the
prepared vegetables and simmer for 5 minutes.
Cook the noodles in boiling water for 5 minutes, then drain
them very thoroughly. Deep fry just before needed in hot oil.
Drain well on absorbent kitchen paper.
Beat the egg with 1 tablespoon of water and pour into a
heated, lightly oiled omelette pan. Make a small omelette and
cut it into thin strips.
To serve, place the noodles on a heated serving dish, top with
the beef mixture and garnish with strips of omelette.
Serves 4-6

Woolly Lamb

This unusual dish owes its name and spectacular appearance to the transparent noodles. If these are not available, substitute 4 ounces of Chinese egg noodles, which should be boiled in water for five minutes, drained and fried.

1 lb. lamb (leg or shoulder)
$\frac{1}{2}$ × 5 oz. can bamboo shoot
1 onion
1 carrot
2 Chinese dried mushrooms
2 tablespoons ($2\frac{1}{2}$ T) peanut oil
$\frac{1}{2}$ teaspoon salt

$\frac{1}{2}$ pint ($1\frac{1}{4}$ cups) chicken stock
1 tablespoon ($1\frac{1}{4}$ T) soy sauce
$\frac{1}{2}$ teaspoon sugar
2 tablespoons ($2\frac{1}{2}$ T) cornflour (cornstarch)
2 oz. Chinese transparent noodles
oil for deep frying

Cut the lamb into thin slices and the bamboo shoot into thin strips. Cut the onion into eighths and the carrot into wedges. Soak the mushrooms in warm water for 20 minutes, rinse, squeeze dry and slice, discarding the stalks.

Heat the oil in a saucepan and fry the meat until it changes colour. Pour off the excess oil and add the prepared vegetables, salt, stock, soy sauce, sugar and cornflour (cornstarch). Bring to the boil and simmer, stirring constantly, for 5 minutes. Loosen the transparent noodles and deep fry in hot oil until they puff up, in about 15 seconds. Drain well on absorbent kitchen paper.

Serve the lamb mixture on a heated serving plate, topped with the noodles.

Serves 4-6

Red Roast Pork

1 lb. pork fillet
1 tablespoon (1¼ T) hoi sin
  sauce
1 teaspoon five-spice powder
1 tablespoon (1¼ T) soy sauce
½ tablespoon soft brown
  sugar

1 clove garlic, crushed
1 teaspoon very finely
  chopped fresh ginger
peanut oil

Trim the pork but leave it in one piece. Mix together all the remaining ingredients except the oil and combine them thoroughly.

Place the meat in a dish, brush it with oil and then coat it in sauce. Marinate the pork for 1-2 hours.

Spoon more oil over the pork, place on a rack in a roasting pan and roast in a hot oven (425°F, Mark 6) for 10 minutes. Reduce the oven temperature to moderate (350°F, Mark 4) for 30-35 minutes.

Cut the fillet in slices diagonally and serve on a hot plate.

Note: Other cuts of pork may be roasted with this sauce. Adjust the roasting time, allowing 35 minutes per pound.

Serves 4-6

Beef with Vegetables

½ lb. topside or rump steak
1 × 5 oz. can bamboo shoot
6 water chestnuts
1 onion
2 sticks celery
1 carrot
2 oz. button mushrooms
1 teaspoon very finely
   chopped fresh ginger

1 tablespoon (1¼ T) sherry
1 teaspoon sugar
½ tablespoon soy sauce
1 tablespoon (1¼ T) cornflour
   (cornstarch)
2 tablespoons (2½ T) peanut oil
1 clove garlic
¼ pint (⅝ cup) beef stock
salt and pepper

Cut the steak into thin strips, about 2 inches × ¼ inch × ¼ inch.
Cut the bamboo shoot into thin strips and slice the water
chestnuts. Cut the onion into eighths. Slice the celery and
carrot diagonally. Cut large mushrooms in half. Mix together
the ginger, sherry, sugar, soy sauce and cornflour (cornstarch).
Heat the oil in a frying pan with the garlic. Fry the garlic until
browned, then remove. Fry the beef until it changes colour,
stirring constantly. Add the soy sauce mixture, stock,
prepared vegetables and seasonings. Bring to the boil, stirring,
and simmer for 5 minutes.
Serve hot.
Serves 4-6

Meat Balls with Pineapple

½ lb. stewing steak (chuck or
   blade)
1 onion
½ egg
salt and pepper
cornflour (cornstarch)
oil for deep frying
½ × 15 oz. can pineapple
   pieces

¼ pint (⅝ cup) syrup from
   canned pineapple
1 tablespoon (1¼ T) cornflour
   (cornstarch)
2 tablespoons (2½ T) vinegar
1 tablespoon (1¼ T) soy sauce
2 tablespoons (2½ T) sugar
green tops of 2 spring onions
   (scallions), chopped

Mince the steak and onion together. Beat the egg lightly and stir it into the meat. Season. Form the mixture into small balls and roll in cornflour (cornstarch). Deep fry them in hot oil until golden.

Place all the remaining ingredients in a saucepan and bring to the boil, stirring constantly. Add the meat balls and simmer, covered, for 5 minutes.

Serve in a heated dish.

Serves 4-6

Red Cooked Beef

2 lb. topside (round or chuck) steak (in one piece)
1 tablespoon ($1\frac{1}{4}$ T) oil
1 tablespoon ($1\frac{1}{4}$ T) soy sauce
1 tablespoon ($1\frac{1}{4}$ T) hoi sin sauce
1 teaspoon sugar
1 teaspoon salt
pinch of pepper

1 teaspoon finely chopped fresh ginger
1 clove garlic, crushed
2 spring onions (scallions), chopped
1 teaspoon sesame seeds
1 tablespoon ($1\frac{1}{4}$ T) sherry

Trim any excess fat from the meat. Heat the oil in a large saucepan and brown the meat all over. Add all the remaining ingredients and enough water just to cover the meat. Bring to the boil and simmer for 2-$2\frac{1}{2}$ hours or until very tender.

Carve the meat into thick slices and pour the gravy over.

Serves 6-8

Sweet and Sour Spareribs

Sweet and sour spareribs should be eaten with the fingers. Supply finger bowls filled with cold water.

3 lb. pork spareribs
½ pint (1¼ cups) vinegar
3 oz. (¾ cup) cornflour
   (cornstarch)
2 tablespoons (2½ T) honey
1 tablespoon (1¼ T) soy sauce
oil for frying
¼ pint (⅝ cup) syrup from

   canned pineapple
2 tablespoons (2½ T) brown
   sugar
½ teaspoon salt
4 pineapple rings
1 onion
1 red pepper

Cut the spareribs into individual ribs, chopping through the bone if necessary. Half fill a large saucepan with water, add 4 tablespoons of the vinegar and bring to the boil. Add the spareribs and simmer for 20 minutes. Drain.

Place the cornflour (cornstarch), honey and soy sauce in a bowl and mix well. Coat the spareribs in this mixture. Heat about 1 inch of oil in a large frying pan and fry the spareribs until golden. Drain well on absorbent kitchen paper.

Put the pineapple syrup in a large saucepan with ¼ pint (⅝ cup) water, brown sugar, salt and the remaining vinegar. Bring to the boil, add the spareribs, cover and simmer for 30 minutes, turning occasionally. Add the pineapple and vegetables to the pan 5 minutes before the cooking time is finished.

Serve hot.

Serves 4-6

SWEET AND SOUR SPARE RIBS (*Photograph: Gales Honey*)

Lamb with Bean Sprouts

½ lb. lamb (shoulder or leg)
1 × 16 oz. can bean sprouts
2 spring onions (scallions)
1 tablespoon (1¼ T) soy sauce
2 tablespoons (2½ T) vinegar
2 tablespoons (2½ T) brown
   sugar
1 teaspoon very finely
   chopped fresh ginger
salt and pepper
1 tablespoon (1¼ T) cornflour
   (cornstarch)
1 tablespoon (1¼ T) peanut oil

Cut the lamb in very thin slices. Drain the bean sprouts, rinse under cold running water and drain again. Cut the spring onions (scallions) into ½ inch lengths. Mix together the soy sauce, vinegar, brown sugar, ginger, salt and pepper, cornflour (cornstarch) and ¼ pint (⅝ cup) water.

Heat the peanut oil in a frying pan and fry the lamb, stirring, until it changes colour. Stir the cornflour (cornstarch) mixture and add to the pan with the spring onions (scallions). Bring to the boil, stirring, and simmer for 2-3 minutes. Add the bean sprouts and cook for a further 2-3 minutes. Serve hot.

Serves 4-6

Shredded Lamb with Onions

1 lb. lean lamb (shoulder or
   leg)
4 onions
1 clove garlic, crushed
1 tablespoon (1¼ T) soy sauce
1 tablespoon (1¼ T) dry sherry
¼ pint (⅝ cup) chicken stock
1 tablespoon (1¼ T) cornflour
   (cornstarch)
1 teaspoon salt
2 tablespoons (2½ T) peanut oil

Cut the lamb into long thin strips. Slice the onions into ⅛ inch rounds. Mix together the garlic, soy sauce, sherry, stock, cornflour (cornstarch) and salt.

Heat the oil in a saucepan and fry the lamb until it changes colour. Stir the cornflour (cornstarch) mixture and add it to the pan with the onions. Bring to the boil, stirring, and simmer for 2-3 minutes. Serve very hot.

Serves 4-6

Spiced Lamb with Vegetables

¾ lb. lamb (shoulder or leg)
1 egg
2 tablespoons (2½ T) cornflour
   (cornstarch)
oil for deep frying
1 red pepper
1 onion
2 sticks celery
1 × 5 oz. can bamboo shoot
1 tablespoon (1¼ T) soy sauce

1 teaspoon hoi sin sauce
1 teaspoon very finely
   chopped fresh ginger
1 clove garlic, crushed
pinch of monosodium
   glutamate
extra 1 tablespoon cornflour
   (cornstarch)
salt

Cut the lamb into thin strips, about 2 inches × ¼ inch × ¼ inch.
Beat the egg and cornflour (cornstarch) together, add the lamb
and stir to coat. Drain off any excess egg, then deep fry the
meat until golden. Drain well on absorbent kitchen paper.
Cut the pepper into wedges and the onion into eighths. Drop
the pepper and onion into boiling water and cook 5 minutes,
drain. Slice the celery diagonally and the bamboo shoot into
thin strips.
Mix together in a saucepan, the soy sauce, hoi sin sauce,
ginger, garlic, monosodium glutamate, salt, the extra cornflour
(cornstarch) and ¼ pint (⅝ cup) of water. Bring to the boil,
stirring constantly, add the vegetables and simmer for 2-3
minutes. Add the lamb and reheat.
Serve in a heated serving dish.
Serves 4-6

Poultry

At least one and often two poultry dishes are included in a Chinese menu. As the cooking time is usually very short, buy young birds whenever possible. When the recipe requires the bird to be boiled first, it is sometimes more economical to use a boiling fowl, which must then be cooked for long enough to ensure that the meat is very tender.

Sweet and Sour Chicken Drumsticks

6 chicken drumsticks
1 egg
4 tablespoons (5 T) cornflour (cornstarch)
salt and pepper
1 onion
1 small pepper
1 carrot
¾ pint (approx. 2 cups) chicken stock

4 tablespoons (5 T) vinegar
4 tablespoons (5 T) soft brown sugar
1 tablespoon (1¼ T) cornflour (cornstarch)
1 tablespoon (1¼ T) soy sauce
1 tablespoon (1¼ T) sherry (optional)
oil for deep frying

Trim the drumsticks if necessary. Beat the egg with 1 tablespoon of water. Mix the cornflour (cornstarch) with salt and pepper. Dip the drumsticks in egg, then in cornflour (cornstarch) and put to one side.

Cut the onion into eighths and the pepper and carrot into wedges. Drop these into a small saucepan of boiling water and cook for 5 minutes. Drain well. Mix together, in a small saucepan, the chicken stock, vinegar, sugar, cornflour (cornstarch), soy sauce and sherry. Bring to the boil, stirring constantly, and simmer for 2-3 minutes.

Heat the oil in a deep frying pan and fry the chicken drumsticks until golden and tender. Drain on absorbent kitchen paper. Add the vegetables to the sauce and then add the chicken. Reheat. Serve hot.

Serves 6

Braised Chicken with Vegetables

A little finely minced barbecued pork is delicious added to this recipe, if available.

1 × 2½ lb. chicken
3 tablespoons (3¾ T) soy sauce
1 tablespoon (1¼ T) dry sherry
  (optional)
½ teaspoon sugar
1 teaspoon salt
1 pineapple ring
1 small pepper
1 carrot
1 stick celery
3 water chestnuts
2 tablespoons (2½ T) peanut
  oil

2 cloves garlic, crushed
1 teaspoon very finely
  chopped fresh ginger
¾ pint (approx. 2 cups)
  chicken stock
1 spring onion, sliced
4 oz. spinach, finely shredded
1 tablespoon (1¼ T) brown
  sugar
1½ (2 T) tablespoons cornflour
  (cornstarch)

Joint the chicken and cut each joint in half to make 8 pieces. Mix together the soy sauce, sherry, sugar and salt. Rub this all over the pieces of chicken and leave for at least 20 minutes. Cut the pineapple into eighths and the pepper and carrot into wedges. Drop these into a small saucepan of boiling water, cook for 5 minutes, and drain. Cut the celery diagonally and slice the water chestnuts into thin rounds.

Heat the oil in a frying pan and add the garlic and ginger. Fry, stirring, for 2 minutes. Add the chicken pieces and brown them all over. Pour off excess oil, add the chicken stock, bring to the boil and simmer, covered, for 30 minutes. Add the pineapple and vegetables to the pan and continue cooking until the chicken is very tender.

Arrange the chicken on a hot serving dish. Mix the sugar and cornflour (cornstarch) with a little water and add to the cooking liquid. Bring to the boil, stirring constantly and cook for 2-3 minutes. Adjust the seasoning. Serve with the sauce poured over the chicken.

Serves 4-6

Chicken with Lychees

1 × 2½ lb. chicken
2 tablespoons (2½ T) soy
   sauce
1 tablespoon (1¼ T) brown
   sugar
3 tablespoons (3¾ T) cornflour
   cornstarch)
salt

1 onion
1 small pepper
2 Chinese dried mushrooms
1 × 11 oz. can lychees
2 tablespoons (2½ T) vinegar
2 tablespoons (2½ T) oil
1 clove garlic, crushed

Place the chicken in a large saucepan and add water to come
halfway up the sides of the chicken. Cook until tender (about
1 hour for a young bird and up to 3 hours for a boiling fowl).
Skin the chicken and remove the flesh from the bones. Cut
the meat into 2-inch squares. Mix together 1 tablespoon of the
soy sauce, brown sugar, 2 tablespoons of the cornflour
(cornstarch) and salt. Add the chicken and marinate for 30
minutes.

Cut the onion into eighths and the pepper into wedges. Put
these in a small saucepan of boiling water, cook for 5 minutes,
and drain. Soak the mushrooms in warm water for 20 minutes,
squeeze dry, and rinse, and slice thinly, discarding the stalks.
Strain the lychees, reserving the syrup. Add enough water to
this syrup to make ½ pint (1¼ cup) of liquid, and combine this
with the vinegar and remaining soy sauce.

Heat 1 tablespoon of the oil with the garlic, fry until golden
and then remove the garlic. Fry the mushrooms for 2 minutes,
add the lychee syrup mixture, bring to the boil and simmer for
2 minutes. Mix the remaining cornflour (cornstarch) with a
little water, add to the pan and boil, stirring, for 2-3 minutes.
Season to taste.

Drain the chicken and deep fry in hot oil until golden. Drain
on absorbent kitchen paper. Add the vegetables and lychees
to sauce and reheat. Arrange the chicken on a warm serving
dish and pour the sauce over.
Serves 4-6

Chicken with Celery and Pineapple Sauce

1 × 2½ lb. chicken
2 sticks celery
3 pineapple rings
1 tablespoon (1¼ T) cornflour
   cornstarch)
1 tablespoon (1¼ T) soy sauce
½ teaspoon very finely
   chopped fresh ginger
4 tablespoons (5 T) pineapple

syrup (from can)
4 tablespoons (5 T) brown
   sugar
4 tablespoons (5 T) vinegar
salt and pepper
1 egg
extra cornflour (cornstarch)
oil for deep frying

Place the chicken in a large saucepan and cover with water.
Bring to the boil then simmer until tender. (This will be about
1 hour for a young bird or 2-3 hours for a boiling fowl.) Drain
and allow to cool.

Cut the celery into diagonal slices and the pineapple rings into
wedges. In a saucepan, mix together the cornflour (cornstarch),
soy sauce and ginger with 4 tablespoons of water, pineapple
syrup and sugar. Bring to the boil, stirring constantly, stir in
the vinegar and cook for 2 minutes. Remove from the heat and
add celery and pineapple wedges. Season to taste.

Disjoint the cooled chicken and cut each joint in half to make
8 pieces. Beat the egg with the salt and pepper. Dip the
chicken pieces in egg and then in cornflour (cornstarch).
Shake off the excess cornflour (cornstarch). Deep fry the
chicken in hot oil until golden.

Arrange the chicken on a serving dish. Reheat the sauce and
pour it over the chicken pieces. Serve hot.

Serves 4-6

Chicken Salad

1 × 2 lb. chicken
1 teaspoon sesame seeds
1 teaspoon very finely
   chopped fresh ginger
2 tablespoons (2½ T) soy sauce
1 clove garlic, crushed
3 tablespoons (3¾ T) sugar
½ teaspoon five-spice powder

oil for deep frying
4 spring onions (scallions)
1 stick celery
6 water chestnuts
1 × 5 oz. can bamboo shoot
salt and pepper
6 lettuce leaves

Joint the chicken. Put the sesame seeds in a small pan and heat gently over a low heat, stirring, until they are toasted golden brown. Crush the ginger and mix with the soy sauce, garlic, sugar and ½ the five-spice powder. Pour this over the chicken and leave for 20 minutes, turning once.

Drain the chicken and fry it in deep hot oil until tender. Drain well on absorbent kitchen paper. Cool, then remove the meat from the bones and cut it into strips. Chill.

Cut the spring onions (scallions) into 1 inch lengths, slice the celery and water chestnuts and cut the bamboo shoot into thin matchstick strips. Mix the chicken with the rest of the five-spice powder and the vegetables. Toss all together lightly. Season. Line a mixing bowl with lettuce leaves. Place the chicken salad in the bowl and sprinkle with a little oil and the toasted sesame seeds.

Serves 4

Satin Chicken

1 × 4 lb. chicken
1 × 5 oz. can bamboo shoot
2 tablespoons (2½ T) soy sauce
2 cloves star anise
1 tablespoon (1¼ T) sherry
½ teaspoon salt
1 clove garlic, crushed

1 teaspoon very finely
   chopped fresh ginger
2 tablespoons (2½ T) peanut oil
¼ pint (⅝ cup) chicken stock
1 tablespoon (1¼ T) cornflour
   (cornstarch)
½ teaspoon sugar

Joint the chicken. Slice the bamboo shoot thinly.
Mix together the soy sauce, star anise, sherry, salt, ginger

and garlic. Rub this mixture all over the chicken pieces and marinate for 1-2 hours.

Heat the oil in a saucepan. Add the chicken pieces and brown them well all over. Add the bamboo shoot and stock. Cover and cook for 20-30 minutes or until the chicken is very tender. Remove the chicken from the bones and cut the meat into long shreds. Mix the cornflour (cornstarch) and sugar with 3 tablespoons ($\frac{1}{4}$ cup) water. Add to the saucepan, bring to the boil, stirring, and simmer for 2-3 minutes. Return the chicken to the saucepan and reheat. Serve in a heated serving bowl.

Serves 4-6

Chicken Chop Suey

4 Chinese dried mushrooms
1 × 5 oz. can bamboo shoot
1 onion
1 pepper
1 × 16 oz. can bean sprouts
12 oz. (3 cups) cooked chicken
2 tablespoons ($2\frac{1}{2}$ T) peanut oil
$\frac{1}{2}$ pint ($1\frac{1}{4}$ cups) chicken stock
$\frac{1}{2}$ teaspoon sugar
1 teaspoon soy sauce
salt and pepper to taste
1 teaspoon cornflour
   (cornstarch)
1 tablespoon ($1\frac{1}{4}$ T) dry sherry

Soak the mushrooms in warm water for 20 minutes, rinse, squeeze dry and cut into thin slices, discarding the stalks. Cut the bamboo shoot into thin strips. Cut the onion into eighths. Slice pepper thinly. Drain the bean sprouts, rinse in cold running water and drain again. Cut the chicken into $\frac{1}{2}$ inch cubes.

Heat the oil in a saucepan and add the chicken and vegetables. Cook, stirring, for 3-4 minutes. Add the stock, sugar, soy sauce and seasonings, bring to the boil, stirring constantly, and simmer for 5 minutes. Mix the cornflour (cornstarch) with sherry and add to the saucepan. Bring to the boil, stirring constantly, and cook for a further 3 minutes.

Serve hot.

Serves 4-6

Crisp Skin Chicken

This dish is eaten with the fingers so place finger bowls of cold water on the table.

1 × 2½ lb. chicken
1 tablespoon (1¼ T) vinegar
2 tablespoons (2½ T) soy sauce
2 tablespoons (2½ T) honey
1 tablespoon (1¼ T) sherry

1 teaspoon treacle
2 tablespoons (2½ T) plain
 flour
1 teaspoon salt
peanut oil for deep frying

Put the chicken into a large saucepan and add boiling water to come halfway up the sides of the chicken. Cover tightly and simmer until just tender, about 45 minutes to 1 hour. Drain, rinse under cold water and dry with kitchen paper.

Mix together the vinegar, soy sauce, honey, sherry and treacle. Brush this all over the chicken and then hang the chicken in an airy place to dry, for about 30 minutes. Brush over the remaining soy sauce mixture and hang again for 20-30 minutes. Mix the flour and salt together and rub well into the chicken skin. Fry in deep hot peanut oil until golden and crisp. Drain well on absorbent kitchen paper.

Chop the chicken into 8 pieces and serve warm with the following dips.

Cinnamon Dip: Mix together 1 tablespoon ground cinnamon, ½ teaspoon ground ginger, ¼ teaspoon each freshly ground black pepper and salt. Place in a small saucepan and heat until very hot, stirring constantly.

Pepper and Salt Dip: Mix together 1 tablespoon salt, and ½ tablespoon freshly ground black pepper. Place in a small saucepan and heat, stirring, until the salt begins to brown.

Hoi Sin Sauce
Guests dip the pieces of chicken into the dips which are served separately in small bowls.
Serves 4-6

CRISP SKIN CHICKEN IN PREPARATION (*Photograph: Gales Honey*)

Braised Duck with Sweet and Pungent Sauce

1 x 4 lb. duck
salt
1 clove garlic, crushed
3 spring onions (scallions), very finely chopped
3 tablespoons (3¾ T) soy sauce
2 tablespoons (2½ T) sherry
2 tablespoons (2½ T) honey

Sauce:
1 small green pepper
1 x 5 oz. can bamboo shoot
2 Chinese dried mushrooms
1 teaspoon finely chopped fresh ginger
1 clove garlic, crushed

2 tablespoons (2½ T) oil
¼ pint (⅝ cup) stock
2 tablespoons (2½ T) honey
¼ pint (⅝ cup) pineapple juice
2 tablespoons (2½ T) vinegar
1 teaspoon tomato paste
1 tablespoon (1¼ T) dry sherry (optional)
1 tablespoon (1¼ T) soy sauce
salt and pepper
2 tablespoons (2½ T) cornflour (cornstarch)
1 x 11 oz. can mandarin oranges
4 pineapple rings, chopped

Wipe the duck inside and out with a damp cloth and rub it all over with salt. Mix the garlic, spring onions (scallions), soy sauce and sherry together. Divide this mixture into 2 and mix honey into one half. Rub the outside of the duck with some of the honey mixture and allow to dry.

Place the duck on a rack in a roasting pan and pour the soy sauce (*not* the honey) mixture inside. Pour 2 inches of water into the roasting pan and cook the duck in a moderate oven (350°F, Mark 4) for 1¾-2 hours or until tender, with the flesh coming away from the bones easily. Add ½ pint (1¼ cups) of boiling water to the honey mixture and baste with this every 20 minutes.

Sauce: Cut the pepper into wedges and the bamboo shoot into thin strips. Soak the mushrooms in warm water for 20 minutes, rinse, squeeze dry and slice, discarding the stalks. Place the oil in a saucepan and fry the prepared vegetables with the ginger and garlic for 5 minutes. Add the stock and bring to the boil. Add the honey, pineapple juice and vinegar, bring to the boil again and stir until the honey has melted. Stir in the tomato paste, sherry, soy sauce and salt and pepper to taste. Mix the cornflour (cornstarch) with a little water and add to the pan. Bring to the boil, stirring constantly and simmer for 2-3 minutes.

Garnish the duck with the mandarin orange segments and pineapple wedges. Pour the sauce over the duck and serve hot.

Note: Make the stock from the duck giblets or use a chicken stock cube.

Serves 4-6

Crisp Duck with Five Spices

Supply finger bowls of cold water as this dish is eaten with the fingers.

1 × 4 lb. duck
2 tablespoons (2½ T) soy sauce
2 cloves star anise
1 teaspoon salt
1 tablespoon (1¼ T) brown
   sugar
2 teaspoons five-spice powder
1 tablespoon (1¼ T) salted

black beans
1 tablespoon (1¼ T) sherry
1 tablespoon (1¼ T) cornflour
   (cornstarch)
1 tablespoon (1¼ T) plain flour
peanut oil for deep frying
fruit chutney for serving

Place the duck in a large saucepan and add 1½ pints (3¾ cups) of water, the soy sauce, star anise, salt, and brown sugar. Bring to the boil and simmer until tender, about 2 hours. Drain the duck well and dry with absorbent kitchen paper. Mix the five spice powder with the beans and sherry and mash very thoroughly. Place 1 teaspoon of the mixture inside the duck and rub the rest over the outside. Sift the flours together and pat on to the outside of the duck. Deep fry the duck in hot oil until golden and crisp. Drain well on kitchen paper.

Chop into eighths through the bones and serve warm with a fruit chutney.

Serves 4-6

Eggs

Eggs are popular in China and are cooked in a very wide variety of ways. Egg dishes have always been a great favourite in Chinese restaurants and are extremely simple to cook at home. Besides being served as part of a meal, they are ideal for unusual supper dishes and snacks.

Prawn (Shrimp) Omelettes

This dish is good served as part of a meal, as an appetizer before the main course or simply as a snack. It can also be made as one large omelette and cut into serving pieces.

4 eggs
1 spring onion (scallion)
2 oz. ($\frac{1}{2}$ cup) prawns (shrimps)
salt
pinch of monosodium
   glutamate

6 fl. oz. ($\frac{3}{4}$ cup) chicken stock
oil for frying
1 tablespoon ($1\frac{1}{4}$ T) soy sauce
1 tablespoon ($1\frac{1}{4}$ T) cornflour
   (cornstarch)
1 teaspoon sugar

Beat the eggs and chop the spring onion (scallion) finely. Mix the eggs with the prawns (shrimps), onion, pinch of salt, monosodium glutamate and 2 tablespoons of the chicken stock. Heat a little oil in a small pan, add $\frac{1}{4}$ of the mixture and fry until golden underneath, stirring occasionally with a fork. Fold in half and keep warm on a plate. Make 3 more omelettes. Place all the remaining ingredients in a saucepan, bring to the boil, stirring constantly, and simmer for 2-3 minutes. Pour the sauce over the omelette and serve immediately.
Serves 4

PRAWN CHOP SUEY. SWEET AND SOUR PRAWNS.
PRAWN OMELETTE (*Photograph: Young's Seafoods*)

Egg Pouch Omelettes

¼ lb. (1 cup) minced (ground) cooked pork

4 spring onions (scallions), finely chopped

1 tablespoon (1¼ T) soy sauce

salt, pepper

1 tablespoon (1¼ T) peanut oil

½ teaspoon sugar

½ teaspoon very finely chopped fresh ginger

1 tablespoon (1¼ T) cornflour (cornstarch)

1 tablespoon (1¼ T) sherry (optional)

4 eggs

oil

¼ pint (⅝ cup) chicken stock

1 extra tablespoon (1¼ T) soy sauce

1 extra tablespoon (1¼ T) cornflour (cornstarch)

Mix together in a bowl the pork, spring onions (scallions), soy sauce, salt, pepper, peanut oil, sugar, ginger, cornflour (cornstarch) and sherry. Beat the eggs.

Heat a little oil in a small omelette pan, pour in a large tablespoon of beaten egg and make a small plain omelette. While the egg is still moist on top, put a teaspoon of the pork mixture in the middle, fold the omelette over and press the edges lightly together. Remove to a serving dish and keep hot. Continue cooking in this way until all the egg is used. Place the chicken stock, and extra soy sauce and cornflour (cornstarch) in a small saucepan. Bring to the boil, stirring, and simmer for 2-3 minutes. Pour over the omelettes and serve immediately.

Serves 4-6

Eggs and Scallops

This dish is suitable for serving as an appetizer as well as part of the main course.

8 oz. scallops

½ × 16 oz. can bean sprouts

3 spring onions (scallions)

5 eggs

salt and pepper

1 tablespoon (1¼ T) peanut oil

Cut the scallops into small pieces. Drain the bean sprouts, rinse under cold running water, and drain again. Chop the

spring onions (scallions) finely. Beat the eggs and season them. Heat the oil in a small frying pan, add the scallops and cook gently for 2-3 minutes. Add the eggs and cook quickly, stirring with a fork occasionally, until just set. Sprinkle the spring onions (scallions) on top and serve, folded, on a heated dish.
Serves 4-6

Mixed Omelette

3 eggs
$\frac{1}{2}$ teaspoon salt
2 tablespoons ($2\frac{1}{2}$ T) cooked or frozen peas
1 red pepper
2 spring onions (scallions)

1 tablespoon ($1\frac{1}{4}$ T) peanut oil
$\frac{1}{4}$ lb. ($\frac{1}{2}$ cup) minced lean pork
$\frac{1}{2}$ tablespoon dry sherry, optional
$\frac{1}{2}$ tablespoon soy sauce
pinch of sugar

Beat the eggs with salt and add the peas. Cut the pepper into matchstick strips and cook in boiling water for 5 minutes. Cut the spring onions (scallions) into thin slices. Add the pepper and spring onions (scallions) to the eggs.
Heat the oil in a frying pan, add the pork and cook, stirring until the colour changes. Pour the eggs into the pan, cook for 1 minute, and add the sherry, soy sauce and sugar. Continue cooking until the omelette is cooked but still moist on top. Serve immediately, on a heated serving dish.
Serves 4-6

Liang-Far Eggs

2 Chinese dried mushrooms
4 oz. Chinese cabbage or spinach
4 sticks celery
1 × 5 oz. can bamboo shoot
2 teaspoons soy sauce
1 tablespoon (1¼ T) dry sherry
½ teaspoon sugar
¼ pint (⅝ cup) chicken stock
1 tablespoon (1¼ T) cornflour
   (cornstarch)

pinch of monosodium
   glutamate
oil for frying
1 clove garlic, crushed
½ teaspoon salt
6 eggs
lettuce for serving

Soak the mushrooms in warm water for 20 minutes, rinse, squeeze dry and slice thinly, discarding the stalks. Shred the cabbage finely. Cut the celery diagonally. Cut the bamboo shoot into thin strips. Mix together the soy sauce, sherry, sugar, stock, cornflour (cornstarch) and monosodium glutamate. Heat 1 tablespoon of oil in a saucepan with the garlic and salt. Add the prepared vegetables and continue cooking, stirring, for 2-3 minutes. Stir the cornflour (cornstarch) mixture and add to the pan. Bring to the boil, stirring constantly, and simmer for 2-3 minutes. Keep hot.

Heat about one inch of oil in a small frying pan. Fry the eggs. Arrange the lettuce on a serving dish, put the eggs on top and pour the sauce over. Serve immediately.

Serves 6

Egg Rolls (Spring Rolls)

The filling can be varied – try substituting bean sprouts (rinsed in cold water and drained) instead of cabbage and prawns (shrimps) (finely chopped) instead of pork.

4 Chinese dried mushrooms
2 spring onions (scallions)
4 water chestnuts
4 oz. finely shredded Chinese
   cabbage or spinach
peanut oil
4 oz. ($\frac{1}{2}$ cup) minced (ground)
   lean pork

4 oz. (1 cup) minced (ground)
   cooked chicken
cornflour (cornstarch)
1 teaspoon soy sauce
4 oz. (1 cup) plain flour
pinch of salt
1 egg
oil for deep frying

Soak the mushrooms in warm water for 20 minutes, rinse, squeeze dry and chop very finely, discarding the stalks. Chop the spring onions (scallions) and water chestnuts finely. Cook the cabbage in 2 tablespoons of boiling water for 2 minutes and drain very well. Heat 1 tablespoon ($1\frac{1}{4}$ T) peanut oil and fry the pork, mushrooms and spring onions (scallions), stirring constantly, for 5 minutes. Add the chicken, water chestnuts, cabbage, 1 teaspoon of cornflour (cornstarch) and soy sauce and mix very well. Put aside to get cold.

Sift 2 oz. ($\frac{1}{2}$ cup) cornflour (cornstarch), plain flour and salt into a mixing bowl. Make a well in the centre and drop in the egg. Using a wooden spoon, mix a little flour into the egg. Gradually add 7 fl. oz. ($\frac{7}{8}$ cup) of water, slowly mixing in the flour. Beat well.

Heat a little oil in a small 6 or 7 inch omelette pan. Pour in enough batter to make a thin layer, cook on one side only then remove to a plate. Continue making pancakes until all the batter is used. Stack the pancakes one on top of the other. Divide the filling between the pancakes, placing it on the cooked side. Roll up the pancakes and tuck in the ends firmly. Seal them well with a cornflour (cornstarch) and water paste. Deep fry in hot oil until golden and drain well on absorbent kitchen paper. Serve piled onto a hot serving plate.

Serves 6-8

Prawn (Shrimp) and Mushroom Omelette

4 oz. (1 cup) peeled prawns
  (shrimps)
4 Chinese dried mushrooms
$\frac{1}{2}$ × 16 oz. can bean sprouts
$\frac{1}{2}$ teaspoon very finely
  chopped fresh ginger

1 tablespoon ($1\frac{1}{4}$ T) sherry
2 tablespoons ($2\frac{1}{2}$ T) chicken
  stock
salt and pepper
4 eggs
oil for frying

Chop the prawns (shrimps). Soak the mushrooms in warm water for 20 minutes, rinse, squeeze dry and slice thinly, discarding the stalks. Drain the bean sprouts, rinse in cold running water and drain again.

Mix together in a saucepan the ginger, sherry, stock and seasonings. Add the prawns (shrimps) and vegetables, cover the pan and heat very gently for 5-7 minutes.

Beat the eggs with 1 tablespoon of water. Heat a little oil in an omelette pan, add the eggs and cook, stirring with a fork, until almost set. Put the prawn (shrimp) mixture in the centre and fold the omelette over.

Lift carefully on to a heated serving plate and serve immediately.

Serves 4-6

Preserved Chinese Eggs

Chinese preserved eggs are sold in shops which specialize in Chinese foods. They look very unappetizing but can make an unusual addition to a Chinese meal or can be served as an appetizer before the main course.

The grey coating of clay and rice husks is cracked and carefully removed. The eggs are then cut into quarters lengthways and are good served with Chinese mixed pickles, soy sauce and finely chopped fresh ginger.

Sweet and Sour Eggs

4 water chestnuts
1 carrot
$\frac{1}{4}$ pint ($\frac{5}{8}$ cup) chicken stock
1 clove garlic, crushed
1 tablespoon ($1\frac{1}{4}$ T) peanut oil
2 tablespoons ($2\frac{1}{2}$ T) sugar
2 tablespoons ($2\frac{1}{2}$ T) vinegar

1 teaspoon tomato paste
$\frac{1}{2}$ teaspoon salt
1 tablespoon ($1\frac{1}{4}$ T) cornflour
  (cornstarch)
4 eggs
oil for frying

Slice the water chestnuts thinly and the carrot in wedges.
Mix together in a small saucepan the stock, garlic, peanut oil,
sugar, vinegar, tomato paste, salt and cornflour (cornstarch).
Bring to the boil, stirring constantly, then add the vegetables
and simmer for 4–5 minutes.
Beat each egg separately with 1 teaspoon of water. Heat a
little oil in a small omelette pan and make 4 omelettes, one
after the other. Fold the omelettes and place on a serving dish.
Pour the sauce over and serve immediately.
Serves 4

Steamed Eggs with Crab

6 eggs
$\frac{3}{4}$ pint (approx. 2 cups)
  chicken stock
1 teaspoon dry sherry

1 tablespoon ($1\frac{1}{4}$ T) soy sauce
$\frac{1}{2}$ tablespoon peanut oil
4 oz. (1 cup) chopped crab
salt and pepper

Beat the eggs and add all the other ingredients. Pour into an
oiled pudding basin and cover with greaseproof paper and
then a layer of aluminium foil. Tie down securely.
Place in a steamer over gently simmering water for 30–40
minutes or until set. (The tip of a knife when put into the egg
will come out quite clean.)
Serve on a heated dish.
Note: Try using other seafood in this recipe such as prawns
(shrimps) or scallops, instead of crab meat.
Serves 4–6

Vegetable Omelettes with Sweet and Sour Sauce

4 Chinese dried mushrooms
$\frac{1}{2} \times 16$ oz. can bean sprouts
3 sticks celery
2 spring onions (scallions)
4 eggs
1 tablespoon ($1\frac{1}{4}$ T) soy sauce
salt and pepper
2 tablespoons ($2\frac{1}{2}$ T) vinegar
1 tablespoon ($1\frac{1}{4}$ T) sugar
1 tablespoon ($1\frac{1}{4}$ T) tomato
  paste

1 teaspoon cornflour
  (cornstarch)
$\frac{1}{2}$ teaspoon very finely
  chopped fresh ginger
1 red pepper
2 pineapple rings
2 tablespoons ($2\frac{1}{2}$ T) syrup
  from canned pineapple
oil for frying

Soak the mushrooms in warm water for 20 minutes, rinse, squeeze dry and slice thinly, discarding the stalks. Drain the bean sprouts, rinse in cold running water and drain again. Slice the celery diagonally and the spring onions (scallions) into thin rounds. Cook the mushrooms and celery in boiling water for 3 minutes, strain. Beat the eggs and add the soy sauce, salt and pepper, and prepared vegetables.

Mix together in a small saucepan the vinegar, sugar, tomato paste, cornflour (cornstarch) and ginger. Cut the pepper and the pineapple rings into wedges and add them to the saucepan with the pineapple syrup and 2 tablespoons of water. Bring to the boil, stirring constantly, and simmer for 3-4 minutes.

Heat enough oil to cover lightly the base of a small omelette pan. Add a generous tablespoon of the egg mixture and cook rapidly until lightly browned underneath. Place on a heated serving dish and keep hot. Continue cooking until all the egg mixture has been made into small omelettes. Pour the sauce over the omelettes and serve immediately.

Serves 4-6

Scrambled Eggs with Prawns (Shrimps)

4 eggs
8 oz. (2 cups) peeled prawns
   (shrimps)
1 teaspoon chopped fresh
   ginger
1 teaspoon dry sherry

1 teaspoon cornflour
   (cornstarch)
pinch of monosodium
   glutamate
pinch of salt
1 tablespoon (1¼ T) peanut oil

Beat the eggs. Chop the prawns (shrimps) roughly. Crush the ginger with a knife blade and reserve the juice. Add the prawns (shrimps), ginger juice, sherry, cornflour (cornstarch), monosodium glutamate and salt to the eggs.

Heat the oil in a large frying pan, add the egg mixture and cook slowly until firm and lightly tinted underneath. Turn the eggs over and cook the other side until tinted brown.

Serve immediately on a heated dish.

Serves 4

Yellow Flow Eggs

2 Chinese dried mushrooms
5 eggs
2 oz. (½ cup) chopped prawns
   (shrimps)
1 oz. (¼ cup) chopped ham
1 oz. (¼ cup) chopped bamboo
   shoot

2 water chestnuts, chopped
1 tablespoon (1¼ T) cornflour
   (cornstarch)
1 teaspoon dry sherry
   (optional)
pinch of salt
1 tablespoon (1¼ T) peanut oil

Soak the mushrooms in warm water for 20 minutes, rinse, squeeze dry and chop mushrooms, discarding the stalks. Beat the eggs and add prawns (shrimps), ham, vegetables, cornflour (cornstarch), sherry, salt and ¼ pint (⅝ cup) of water.

Heat the oil in a saucepan, add the egg mixture and cook over a low heat, stirring continuously with a wooden spoon, until the eggs have set.

Serve on a heated serving dish.

Serves 4-6

Vegetables

Vegetables are often incorporated in the other savoury recipes in this book but they are also delicious served on their own, or as the main ingredient of a dish. They are always cut up into small pieces which cook very quickly and lend themselves to Chinese cooking methods. The Chinese never over-cook their vegetables – in fact to a Westerner they often appear to be under-cooked as they retain their colour and crispness. Chinese vegetables such as bean sprouts, bamboo shoot and water chestnuts are most easily obtainable canned. Some larger supermarkets, however, do stock some fresh Chinese vegetables – use these whenever possible.

Braised Cabbage with Mushrooms

1 lb. cabbage, or Chinese
   cabbage if available
2 tablespoons (2½ T) peanut oil
1 green pepper
1 tablespoon (1¼ T) soy sauce

1 teaspoon sugar
pinch of monosodium
   glutamate
4 oz. button mushrooms
salt and pepper

Clean the cabbage and chop it roughly. Heat the oil in a saucepan, add the cabbage and fry it for 2-3 minutes, stirring constantly. Cut the pepper into matchstick strips and add these to the pan with the soy sauce, sugar, monosodium glutamate and mushrooms. Season. Add 4 tablespoons of water, cover the pan and cook for 5-7 minutes, shaking the pan occasionally.
Put into a hot serving dish and serve immediately.
Serves 4-6

Sesame and Chicken Salad

1 × 11 oz. can lychees in syrup
6 lettuce leaves or Chinese
   cabbage leaves if available
3 tablespoons (3¾ T) peanut oil
2 tablespoons (2½ T) vinegar
1 tablespoon (1¼ T) toasted
   sesame seeds
1 teaspoon soy sauce
1 teaspoon sugar
pinch of monosodium
   glutamate

½ teaspoon dry mustard
salt and pepper
½ × 5 oz. can bamboo shoot,
   sliced
6 water chestnuts, sliced
3 spring onions (scallions),
   chopped
4 oz. (1 cup) cooked chicken,
   cut in thin strips

Drain the canned lychees. Shred the lettuce and put it in a covered bowl in the refrigerator to get crisp.

Mix together in a bowl the oil, vinegar, sesame seeds, soy sauce, sugar, monosodium glutamate, mustard, salt and pepper. Add the bamboo shoot, water chestnuts and spring onions (scallions) and marinate for 1 hour. Add the lychees and lettuce just before serving, toss lightly and put into a serving bowl. Scatter the chicken strips on top.

Note: Toast sesame seeds by placing them in a dry frying pan and heating very gently, stirring, until golden.

Serves 4-6

Braised Mushrooms

12 Chinese dried mushrooms
¾ pint (approx. 2 cups)
   chicken stock
1 tablespoon (1¼ T) soy sauce
2 spring onions (scallions),
   chopped

1 teaspoon very finely
   chopped fresh ginger
½ tablespoon cornflour
   (cornstarch)

Soak the mushrooms in warm water for 20 minutes, rinse and squeeze dry. Remove and discard the stalks. Pour the chicken stock into a saucepan, bring to the boil, and add the mushrooms, soy sauce, spring onions (scallions) and ginger. Cover and simmer for 1-1½ hours or until the mushrooms are very tender.

Put the mushrooms on to a serving plate and keep them warm. Mix the cornflour (cornstarch) to a paste with a little water and add it to the liquor in pan. Bring to the boil, stirring constantly, and simmer for 2-3 minutes. Pour the sauce over the mushrooms and serve.

Serves 4

Broccoli with Pork

12 oz. cooked or frozen broccoli
2 tablespoons (2½ T) peanut oil
1 teaspoon sugar
pinch of salt
½ teaspoon very finely chopped fresh ginger

1 clove garlic, crushed
2 tablespoons (2½ T) soy sauce
1 tablespoon (1¼ T) sherry
1 teaspoon cornflour (cornstarch)
¼ lb. (1 cup) thinly sliced cooked pork

Cut the broccoli into 1½ inch lengths. Heat the oil in a saucepan, add the broccoli and fry for 2-3 minutes. Add the sugar, salt, ginger and garlic, cover the pan and cook slowly for 4-5 minutes.

Mix the soy sauce, sherry and cornflour (cornstarch) with 3 tablespoons of water. Stir this in to the saucepan, cover again and cook for a further 3-4 minutes. Add the pork and reheat.

Serves 4-6

Bean Sprouts with Spring Onions

1 × 16 oz. can bean sprouts
2 spring onions (scallions)
1 tablespoon (1¼ T) peanut oil
1 clove garlic

¼ pint (⅝ cup) chicken stock
pinch of monosodium glutamate
salt and pepper

Drain the bean sprouts, rinse under cold running water and drain again. Slice the spring onions (scallions) into ½ inch lengths.

Heat the oil with the garlic and fry until golden. Remove and discard the garlic. Add the bean sprouts and onions to pan and fry, stirring continuously, for 3-4 minutes. Add the chicken stock and seasonings, bring to the boil and simmer for 2 minutes. Serve in a heated dish.

Serves 4-6

Rice and Noodles

Rice is the staple diet of the Chinese. It is eaten at every meal. Short-grained rice is most commonly used, but the long-grained rice is often preferred in the Western world. Originally, boiled rice was always served, and fried rice was just a way to use up the cold left-over rice, the next day. Fried rice has now become a dish in its own right with many delicious variations.

Dried noodles are readily available in larger supermarkets, but it is worthwhile, if you have time, either to make your own or to buy fresh noodles from a Chinese food store. The noodle paste can also be used for making dumplings and wun tuns.

Plain Boiled Rice

10 oz. (1¼ cups) rice
1 pint (2 ½ cups) water

2 teaspoons salt

Wash the rice very well in several changes of water. Place the water in a large saucepan with the salt. Bring to the boil, add the rice and bring to boiling point again, stirring with a fork all the time. Cover the saucepan and cook the rice very slowly for 20 minutes. Remove the lid, allow the steam to escape and serve in a heated serving dish.

Note: Do not lift the saucepan lid before cooking time is finished or the steam will escape and the rice will not cook properly. More boiling water will probably have to be added. Cooked properly, the rice will have absorbed all the water by the time it is cooked.

This quantity serves **4-6**. If less rice is required, the amount of water should be adjusted proportionately. Thus for 6 ounces of rice, the same method should be followed, using 12 fluid ounces (1½ cups) of water.

Fried Rice

6 oz. (¾ cup) rice
1 oz. (¼ cup) blanched almonds
1 × 1 oz. slice cooked ham
3 spring onions (scallions)

2 eggs
½ teaspoon salt
2 tablespoons (2½ T) peanut oil
1 tablespoon (1¼ T) soy sauce

Boil the rice (see the previous recipe). Cool, cover and place in the refrigerator or in a cool place overnight.

Split the almonds in half and toast them lightly by placing them in the grill pan under a very hot grill for a few minutes until golden. Stir occasionally and watch that they do not burn.

Cut the ham into long thin strips and chop the spring onions into ¼ inch lengths. Beat the eggs and salt together well.

Heat the oil in a large frying pan. Add the egg and fry until it is half cooked. Add the rice (make sure that there are no lumps) and coat the grains in egg, stirring quickly. Keep stirring and turning the rice over and over. Add the ham and onions and sprinkle in the soy sauce. Fry for 3-4 minutes, stirring constantly.

Serve in a heated serving dish sprinkled with the almonds.

Serves 4-6

Party Fried Rice

6 oz. ($\frac{3}{4}$ cup) rice

1 × 16 oz. can bean sprouts

4 oz. (1 cup) peeled prawns
  (shrimps)

4 oz. (1 cup) cooked chicken

2 eggs

salt

2 tablespoons ($2\frac{1}{2}$ T) peanut oil

1 tablespoon ($1\frac{1}{4}$ T) soy sauce

Cook the rice (see recipe page 82). Cool, cover and place in the refrigerator or a cool place overnight.
Drain the bean sprouts, rinse under cold running water and drain again. Cut any large prawns (shrimps) in half and cut the chicken into strips. Beat the eggs with salt. Heat the oil in a large frying pan. Add the eggs and fry until half set. Add the rice and fry quickly, stirring constantly until the grains are coated in egg. Keep stirring and turning the rice over. Add the prawns (shrimps), chicken and soy sauce. Fry, stirring constantly, for 3-4 minutes.
Serves 4-6

Noodle Paste

1 egg

8 oz. (2 cups) plain flour

pinch of salt

Sift the flour and salt into a mixing bowl. Make a well in the centre and add the egg. Using a round bladed knife, mix the flour into the egg and then add enough water to make a stiff dough. Knead the dough with the hand, very thoroughly.
Roll out the dough as thinly as possible on a lightly floured board. Use as required.
Wun Tuns: Cut into 2-3 inch squares and use with one of the recipes in this chapter.
Noodles: Lightly flour the dough, roll up like a Swiss roll and slice into 1/16-$\frac{1}{8}$ inch slices. Unroll and hang over the back of a chair (on a clean tea towel) for about 20 minutes, to dry out.
For soft noodles, boil for 5-7 minutes in a large saucepan of boiling salted water.
For crisp noodles, fry in deep hot oil until golden and drain well on absorbent kitchen paper. There is no need to boil the noodles before frying as with bought dried noodles.

Wun Tun

Wun tun skins can be purchased from shops specializing in Chinese groceries. You can however use noodle paste, which should be rolled out thinly and cut into squares. Serve wun tuns as part of the main course with a pungent sauce if liked. They can also be served as an appetizer or a snack.

24 wun tun skins or $\frac{1}{2}$ the recipe for noodle paste, see recipe opposite
8 oz. (2 cups) cooked minced chicken
8 oz. (2 cups) peeled prawns (shrimps)
2 spring onions (scallions)

pinch of sugar
pinch of salt and pepper
pinch of monosodium glutamate
1 tablespoon ($1\frac{1}{4}$ T) soy sauce
egg yolk
oil for deep frying

Mince or chop finely the chicken, prawns (shrimps) and spring onions (scallions). Add the sugar, salt and pepper, monosodium glutamate and soy sauce and mix thoroughly.

Divide this filling evenly between the paste squares. Spread the filling over each square and roll it up, like a Swiss roll, folding in the ends. Seal the edges with egg yolk.

Deep fry in hot oil until golden. Drain well on absorbent kitchen paper and serve as soon as possible with pungent sauce.

Pungent Sauce: Mix together in a small saucepan 2 tablespoons of sugar, 2 tablespoons of vinegar, 1 teaspoon soy sauce, $\frac{1}{2}$ teaspoon very finely chopped fresh ginger, 1 teaspoon tomato paste, $\frac{1}{4}$ teaspoon salt, $\frac{1}{4}$ pint ($\frac{5}{8}$ cup) water and 1 tablespoon cornflour (cornstarch).

Bring to the boil, stirring constantly, and simmer for 2-3 minutes.

Note: Wun tuns when made by the Chinese are folded in a very complicated manner. This recipe and rolling of the wun tuns will save a lot of time and tastes very good.

Serves 6-8

Desserts

The Chinese usually like to finish a meal with some fresh fruit. This may be lychees, loquats or longans, but melon, bananas, apples, pears and mandarin oranges are also eaten. For a feast or special occasion, however, there are some light desserts and biscuits which may be served to complete the meal.

Almond Cream with Chow Chow

Chow chow is Chinese preserved fruit which can be bought in shops specializing in Chinese groceries.

1 × 16 oz. can chow chow or mixed fruit salad
1 pint (2½ cups) water
1 oz. (4 tablespoons) gelatine

¾ pint (2 cups) milk
granulated sugar to taste
1 teaspoon almond essence

Chop the larger pieces of chow chow in half or drain the mixed fruit salad.
Place 4 tablespoons of the water in a cup and stand it in a saucepan of hot water. Shower the gelatine into the cup and heat, stirring, until the gelatine has dissolved. Cool.
Heat the remaining water with milk, sugar to taste, and almond essence, stir until the sugar is dissolved. Stir in the gelatine. Pour into a shallow, lightly oiled cake tin and cool until set.
Cut the almond cream into triangular bite-sized pieces. Place these in a serving bowl with the fruit and combine very gently. Serve very cold.
Serves 6-8

Almond Lake with Mandarin Oranges

1 pint (2½ cups) milk
4 oz. (½ cup) granulated sugar
1 teaspoon almond essence
2 oz. (⅓ cup) ground rice
1 × 11 oz. can mandarin
  oranges
1 oz. (¼ cup) flaked toasted
  almonds

Put the milk, sugar, essence and rice into a saucepan. Bring to the boil, stirring constantly, and simmer for 5 minutes. Pour into a dish, cover and cool. Drain the mandarin oranges well. Spoon the rice into individual serving dishes. Place the mandarin oranges on the rice and sprinkle the toasted almonds on top.
Note: Toast the almonds by placing in the grill pan and heating under a hot grill, stirring occasionally, until golden.
Serves 4-6

Gingered Fruit

1 × 15 oz. can pineapple pieces
1 × 11 oz. can lychees
1 tablespoon (1¼ T) chopped
  glacé cherries
2 tablespoons (2½ T) chopped
  crystallized ginger
1 oz. (¼ cup) toasted flaked
  almonds

Drain the syrup from the canned fruits. Lightly combine the pineapple, lychees, glacé cherries and ginger in a serving bowl. Chill well. Sprinkle the almonds on top and serve immediately.
Note: Toast the almonds by spreading the blanched, flaked almonds in the grill pan and heating them, stirring occasionally, until lightly tinted.
Serves 6-8

Mow Flower Twists

8 oz. (2 cups) plain flour
4 oz. ($\frac{1}{2}$ cup) margarine or
  butter
4 oz. ($\frac{1}{2}$ cup) granulated sugar
1 oz. (3 tablespoons) ground
  almonds

1 egg
$\frac{1}{2}$ teaspoon almond essence
oil for deep frying
icing sugar

Sift the flour into a bowl and rub in the margarine or butter
with the fingertips until the mixture resembles breadcrumbs.
Stir in the sugar and ground almonds. Add the egg and essence
and knead very well to make a pliable dough, adding a little
water if necessary.

Roll the dough into a sausage about 1 inch in diameter and cut
off 1 inch lengths. Roll each piece into a ribbon about 9-10
inches long, fold in half and twist twice. Take the ends of the
ribbon back to the fold and push through the loop.

Carefully fry these twists in deep hot oil and cook until
golden. Drain well on absorbent kitchen paper. Sprinkle with
icing sugar. Serve cold.

Makes about 16

Caramel Apples

Other fruit, such as bananas, pears, plums, can also be served in this way.

6 apples
$1\frac{1}{2}$ oz. (6 T) plain flour
$\frac{1}{2}$ oz. (2 T) cornflour
   (cornstarch)
2 egg whites

oil for deep frying
4 oz. ($\frac{1}{2}$ cup) granulated sugar
1 tablespoon ($1\frac{1}{4}$ T) oil
1 tablespoon ($1\frac{1}{4}$ T) sesame seeds

Peel, core and quarter the apples. Dust them lightly with some of the plain flour.
Sift the remaining plain flour with the cornflour (cornstarch) into a mixing bowl. Add the egg whites and mix to a paste. Add the apple quarters and stir to coat in paste. Deep fry in hot oil until golden. Drain well on absorbent kitchen paper. Place the sugar in a small saucepan with 2 tablespoons ($\frac{1}{4}$ cup) water. Heat, stirring, until the sugar has dissolved. Add the oil and continue heating slowly until the sugar has caramelised and is a light golden brown. Stir in the apple and sesame seeds. Serve immediately in individual serving dishes which have been very lightly oiled. A bowl of cold water should also be on the table and the guests pick up their apple with chopsticks or tongs and drop them into the water before eating, for the caramel to harden.
Serves 4-6

CARAMEL APPLES (*Photograph: The Fruit Producers' Council*)

Sesame Biscuits

4 oz. ($\frac{1}{2}$ cup) granulated sugar $\frac{1}{2}$ teaspoon baking powder
4 oz. ($\frac{1}{2}$ cup) margarine or butter   8 oz. (2 cups) plain flour
                                       sesame seeds

Cream the butter and sugar in a bowl until light and soft.
Beat in 1 egg gradually, beating well after each addition. Stir
in the flour sifted with the baking powder.
Place the dough on a lightly floured board and knead lightly.
Form the dough into balls about 1 inch in diameter and flatten
with the palm of the hand.
Separate the remaining egg, beat the yolk lightly and brush it
over the biscuits. Press the egg yolk side of the biscuits into
the sesame seeds and press them on firmly.
Place the biscuits on a lightly oiled baking tray, seed side up,
brush with the egg white and bake in a moderate oven
(350°F, Mark 4) for about 15 minutes or until golden. Cool
on a wire cooling tray. **Makes about 30 biscuits**

Almond Biscuits

12 oz. (3 cups) plain flour   1 egg
2 teaspoons baking powder   1 teaspoon almond essence
pinch of salt   blanched almonds for
4 oz. ($\frac{1}{2}$ cup) margarine or   decoration
   butter   beaten egg for glazing
8 oz. (1 cup) granulated sugar

Sift the flour, baking powder and salt into a bowl. Cream the
margarine and sugar together until light, white and fluffy.
Beat in the egg and almond essence. Stir in the sifted dry
ingredients to make a stiff dough.
Form the mixture into balls about 1-1$\frac{1}{4}$ inch diameter and place
these on a greased baking tray. Place half an almond (split
lengthways) on each ball and press to flatten slightly. Brush
with beaten egg.
Bake in a moderate oven (350°F, Mark 4) for 20 minutes or
until golden. Cool on a wire rack. **Makes about 45 biscuits**

Eight Treasures Rice

6 oz. ($\frac{3}{4}$ cup) short grain rice
4 oz. ($\frac{2}{3}$ cup) brown sugar
2 oz. ($\frac{1}{2}$ cup) dates
2 oz. ($\frac{1}{2}$ cup) blanched
   almonds
2 oz. ($\frac{1}{2}$ cup) walnuts

2 oz. ($\frac{1}{3}$ cup) glacé cherries
2 oz. ($\frac{1}{2}$ cup) mixed peel
2 oz. ($\frac{1}{2}$ cup) raisins
2 oz. ($\frac{1}{3}$ cup) glacé pineapple,
   apricots, or figs as available

Cook the rice in boiling water for about 15 minutes or until tender. Drain and stir in the sugar.

Place a layer of rice in the base of an oiled 1$\frac{1}{2}$-2 pint pudding bowl. Add a layer of fruit and nuts to make a pattern, pressing it through the rice so that it will be seen as decoration when the pudding is unmoulded. Add another layer of rice, then a layer of mixed nuts and fruit. Continue layering until all the ingredients have been used, finishing with a layer of rice.

Press down very firmly and cover with greased greaseproof paper or aluminium foil. Place the bowl in a steamer over gently boiling water, or in a saucepan with simmering water coming halfway up the side of the bowl. Cook for 30-40 minutes. Unmould and serve hot.

Serves 6-8

Index